A History of
GREATER BIRMINGHAM
– down to 1830

Victor Skipp

Published by the author
from 5 Clay Lane, Yardley, Birmingham B26 1DU.

To the Shade of William Hutton
— who was writing the first history of
Birmingham exactly two hundred years ago.

First published 1980

© 1980 Victor H. T. Skipp

Filmset by
Ace Engravers Ltd., 42 Princip Street, Birmingham B4 6LN
Printed by
Rogers (Printers) Birmingham Ltd., 5 Aston Road North, Birmingham B6 4DS

British Library Cataloguing in Publication Data

Skipp, Victor
    A history of Greater Birmingham.
    1. Birmingham, Eng.–History
    I. Title
    942.4′96   DA690.B6

ISBN 0-9506998-0-2

GREATER BIRMINGHAM

WITHDRAWN

Contents

N

PARISH BOUNDARY
CITY & PARISH BOUNDARY
CITY BOUNDARY

SUTTON COLDFIELD

MINWORTH

DETACHED PORTION OF CURDWORTH

ASTON

HANDSWORTH

SHELDON

BIRMINGHAM

LYNDON
DETACHED PORTION OF BICKENHILL

EDGBASTON

YARDLEY

DETACHED PORTION OF HALESOWEN

HARBORNE

QUINTON

KING'S NORTON

NORTHFIELD

0   1   2
MILES

Birmingham and Greater Birmingham

The original township of Birmingham covered slightly under 3,000 acres. Its modern namesake (including Sutton Coldfield) occupies over 65,000 acres and incorporates all or part of twelve other ancient parishes and over twice as many ancient manors.

In the past there has been a tendency for writers on Birmingham to ignore the outlying parts of the city until the date of their take-over. It makes better historical sense, however, to think of the whole of Greater Birmingham from the start. All through the Middle Ages the villages and hamlets of this area must have looked to Birmingham as their principal market centre. When the iron industry began to develop in the sixteenth century nailers and cutlers were to be found at Aston, Bordesley, Yardley and King's Norton, as well as in Leland's 'good market toune'. Two centuries later the slitting, grinding and boring mills used by 'Birmingham' manufacturers lay scattered throughout the Greater Birmingham district, wherever a sufficient head of water could be found. And, as everybody knows, it was not in Birmingham itself but in the neighbouring parish of Handsworth that Boulton and Watt produced their epoch-making steam engines.

Since Tudor times Birmingham has also been closely linked with the Black Country, the once rich coal and iron producing area to its north and west. Not only did the Black Country provide Birmingham craftsmen with their raw materials, many a Birmingham businessman made his fortune by marketing the Black Country's finished products. But despite this industrial and commercial interdependence, Birmingham and the Black Country have always been culturally separate worlds. 'One insult that no Black Countryman will tolerate', says Phil Drabble, 'is to be mistaken for a Brummie.' To which the Brummie Vivian Bird has replied, 'The greatest insult that can be levelled at a Brummie is to equate him with a Black Countryman.'

Birmingham has a character of its own; and it will be part of the aim of this book to show how that character is deeply rooted in its medieval and early modern past.

The 102 square miles of land which is occupied by 'Britain's second city' is situated at the centre of a slightly elevated area known as the Birmingham Plateau and is drained by a 'hand' of small rivers flowing northwards into the Trent. As a result anyone travelling across Birmingham's gently undulating terrain from east to west passes over a succession of watersheds and valleys. The highest of the watersheds is that between the Rea and the Tame: for whereas the others consist of a relatively soft red clay known as Keuper Marl, this one is spined by the much more resistant Keuper Sandstone. It is on this sandstone ridge that the city centre

*Left:
Greater Birmingham and its ancient parishes.*

7

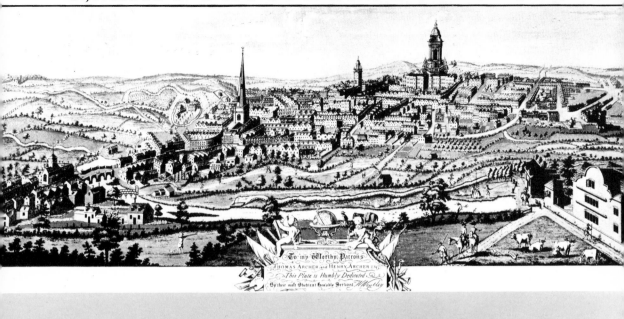

Top:
The East Prospect of Birmingham William Westley, 1732.
Centre:
The East Prospect today (from Bolto Road).
Bottom:
St. Martin's and St. Philip's (no Birmingham Cathedral). These are t only buildings shown on the 173 prospect that survive today.

8

Top:
The River Rea at Deritend Bridge, as
shown on Westley's East Prospect.
Above:
The Rea at the same point today
(Floodgate Street), but looking in the
reverse direction.

stands, dominating the rest of Birmingham on all but its south-western side. 'Except from Halesowen...', says William Hutton, Birmingham's first historian, 'the approach on every side is by ascent.' Westley's well-known eighteenth century prospect brings out this acropolis-like effect admirably; the towering office blocks and hotels of today's 'Manhattanized' skyline make it still more obvious.

The four-mile long Queensway or Inner Ring Road, with its huge traffic 'circuses', girdles part of the sandstone ridge. St. Martin's Circus has the traditional open Bull Ring market at its centre, while just below stands St. Martin's itself, Birmingham's original parish church; and beyond that, Digbeth, running steeply down to the once crucial crossing of the River Rea. Westley's prospect shows this to have been a substantial stream and, like others in the area, we know that it was extremely liable to flood. Nowadays it is difficult to spot in its open concrete conduit even from the top of a bus. Like Wigan pier, the Rea must surely have become a music hall joke, had enough Brummies been aware of its existence.

The Bull Ring, St. Martin's and Digbeth, on the eastern-facing slope of the ridge between the Tame and the Rea, represent Birmingham's medieval nucleus. 'The bewty of Bremischam', wrote Leland about 1540, '...is in one strete goyng up alonge almoste from . . . the broke up a mene hille by the lengthe of a quarter of a mile ...' It was in the early eighteenth century that a new and fashionable extension of the town was draped over the top of the hill; only to be largely replaced in the nineteenth century by the proud civic buildings and shopping streets of the Victorian city; and then, in our own time, by what has been called the 'concrete cubism' of twentieth century Birmingham.

Nevertheless, even after the massive redevelopment programme of the last twenty-five years, a good deal of Birmingham's early history is still there to be 'read' in the streets of the city centre. And the same is just as true elsewhere in Greater Birmingham.

By A.D. 1300 there must have been somewhere between 40 and 50 villages and hamlets inside the modern city boundary. Today these places are just districts of Birmingham. But each was originally a separate little community and enjoyed anything up to a thousand years of separate and independent history, before it was eventually swallowed up by its gargantuan neighbour.

All over Birmingham, indeed, we can still find the remains of these buried villages. At places like Yardley, Sheldon, Northfield and King's Norton, a medieval church continues in use. Most of the settlements had their own manor house; and many of these survive, like Weoley Castle, Selly Manor and Aston Hall. The

village inn may still be there, like the Great Stone Inn at Northfield, with the old village pound still standing close by. At Yardley and King's Norton there are ancient village schools. And in almost every district the odd farmhouse or cottage has escaped destruction, like Stratford Place, which is a Bordesley yeoman's house of the early seventeenth century, or Blakesley Hall at Yardley, which now serves as a local history museum.

Nor does the past reveal itself merely in terms of ancient buildings. Most of the main, and not a few of the minor, roads of Greater Birmingham date back to medieval times: and with them, unfortunately, some of our most frustrating traffic jams, which may be directly traced back to decisions made by local peasants centuries before the motor car was thought of.

Even in places where all else has been swept away by development and redevelopment, the place-names remain to tell their story. To tell us, for instance, that sallows, or willows, were once the dominant tree at Saltley; that Ladywood was once woodland; that Winson Green, Balsall Heath and Short Heath were once grazed by sheep and cattle; or that the River Cole could once only be crossed at Stechford by means of a 'sticky ford'.

This book will trace the history of Birmingham down to about 1830; by which time the town itself had already emerged as a nationally important industrial and commercial centre. But it will also bear in mind the surrounding countryside which was only to be taken over during the rampant urban growth of the following century. For, as we shall see, at every stage, this rural hinterland played an essential part in the making of Birmingham.

Left:
Aston Hall, built for Sir Thomas Ho[lte] between 1618 and 1635.
Above:
The Great Stone Inn at Northfiel[d] with the seventeenth-century (?) villag[e] pound in which stray animals wer[e] kept until their owner had paid th[e] appropriate fine.

10

A Roman Base Camp

On 28 September 1953, under the shadow of the University Medical School and the vast Queen Elizabeth Hospital, the then lord mayor of Birmingham mounted the ramparts of the recently restored north-west corner of Metchley Camp and declared this remnant of the 'oldest construction' in the city officially open to the public. But latter-day Vandals have long since sacked the site, and there is now little left for the visitor to see.

This is a pity, for Birmingham is far from rich in early antiquities. The City Museum has a small collection of Old and Middle Stone Age implements which recall the tens of thousands of years during which the area was occasionally traversed or fitfully occupied by small groups of primitive hunters and food-gatherers. Other, somewhat more sophisticated tools and weapons represent the New Stone Age, whose peoples were Britain's first farmers. These include polished hand axes found at Handsworth, Stirchley and Deritend – the latter perhaps indicating that the River Rea was already being crossed at this fording point as long as 6,000 years ago. However, no Neolithic pottery has been found; nor is there any clear evidence that Neolithic groups actually lived and farmed in the Birmingham district. Bronze Age implements of the earliest type are also lacking, though there are fine bronze axe-heads from 1400-1000 B.C., as well as stone battle axes of a similar date.

The Celtic Iron Age has more to offer. The natural vegetation of the Birmingham Plateau at this time would have been deciduous forest: extremely thick and intractable on the extensive stretches of Keuper Marl, somewhat lighter where this is overlain by patches of glacial drift, and also on the Bunter Pebble Beds which are to be found to the west. Apart from a modest tally of Celtic small finds, it is thought that some of the 'crop sites' which have been detected by aerial photography in the environs of Birmingham may turn out to be Iron Age farmsteads. And certainly, just beyond the 'city boundary, there are two Iron Age hill-forts: the multiple-ramparted Wychbury Camp, near Hagley, and Shirley's 11 acre Berry Mound. Another pointer to the presence of significant Celtic populations – which no doubt persisted and perhaps increased during Roman times – is the fact that two of Birmingham's three principal rivers – the Cole and the Tame – bear Celtic names.

Metchley Camp was established about A.D. 48 by the Roman army as a base camp for its conquest and pacification of the Birmingham area. It stood by the city's earliest known road junction: at the point where the Ryknield Street was met by Roman roads coming in from Droitwich and Penkridge. The

The Lord Mayor of Birmingham (Ald. G. H. W. Griffith) opening Metchley Camp (Birmingham Post and Mail).

course of the former road, which ran from Bourton on the Foss Way to Wall on the Watling Street, passes south-north through the entire length of Greater Birmingham. Moreover, although the modern city has almost entirely obliterated even the line of Ryknield Street, one can still walk for 1½ miles along its often raised 'agger', as it crosses the western side of Sutton Park.

At first the Metchley fort was a rectangular enclosure of 10½ acres, being defended by a double ditch, plus a high earthen bank, topped with a wooden stockade. But a 4 acre extension soon had to be added on the northern side, complete with defensive towers in the north-east and north-west corners. By this time the station was large enough to house about 3,000 troops in substantial timber buildings.

Quite often a Roman military camp led in turn to the development of a civil settlement, or town. This happened locally at Penkridge, Wall, Droitwich and Alcester. But it did not happen here. The 14½ acre fort appears to have been abandoned when the Roman armies advanced westwards in A.D. 57. From about A.D. 80 the site was again under military occupation, the earlier defences being levelled and a 6¼ acre fort constructed inside its predecessor. This smaller camp may have continued in use down to about A.D. 120. But as far as we can tell, that was the end of the Roman story at Metchley.

Elsewhere in Greater Birmingham evidence for life during the Roman occupation is almost entirely limited to Roman coins, which have come to light at about 25 different find-points. In view of the dearth of more substantial remains, the recent discovery little more than a mile beyond the city boundary, at Coleshill, of a major Roman villa and/or temple site has come as a great surprise.

Nevertheless, on present evidence, the Birmingham area as a whole would seem to have remained relatively sparsely inhabited throughout the Roman period; and it looks unlikely that more than a small proportion of its natural woodland could have been cleared prior to the coming of the Anglo-Saxons.

Above:
Ryknield Street, Sutton Park. Th small puddle is in the middle of th 'agger' or carriageway.
Below:
Plan of the Roman forts at Metchle as revealed by excavations carried ou between 1953 and 1968.

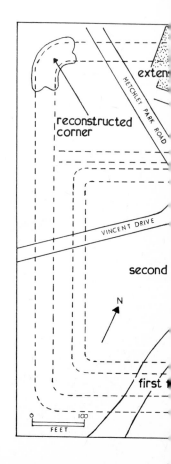

12

Saxon Clearings and Domesday Manors

Although the Anglo-Saxons were relatively late in reaching the central midlands, surviving place-names suggest that their settlement of the Birmingham area was well under way by A.D. 700. Weoley Castle, where 'tantalizing clues to... possibly pre-Norman occupation' underlie the excavated footings of a fortified medieval manor house, bears a name that may go back to the Old English *wēoh-lēah*, meaning 'clearing in which there is a heathen temple'. As such, like Wednesbury ('Wōden's fortress') and Wednesfield ('Wōden's plain') in the upper Tame valley, it could well date from before the conversion of the midlands to Christianity, a process which began in A.D. 653 and is thought to have been fairly rapid. Similarly, the name Birmingham belongs to a group of so-called *'ingāham'* place-names which – though not as early as was once thought – probably passed out of vogue before 700.

Two main tribal groups seem to have been involved in the settlement of the Greater Birmingham area. The Anglian Mercians entered the midlands from the north, initially following the Trent Valley, and then spreading along the valleys of the Tame and its tributaries, the Cole and the Rea, into the centre of the Birmingham Plateau. It was presumably the Mercian people known as *Tomsaetan* ('dwellers by the Tame') who founded Birmingham and other early settlements in the north.

Some of the southern villages, on the other hand, were more likely founded by the Saxon tribal group known as the *Hwicce*. These people approached the midland area from the south, colonizing the lower Severn and lower Avon valleys, and then moving up on to the Birmingham Plateau via the valleys of the Salwarpe, Arrow and Alne. When the Domesday survey was made in 1086 several local settlements undoubtedly had southern connections. Yardley was a dependent manor of Beoley, six miles south in the upper valley of the Arrow, and could well have been founded by prospectors from that place. King's Norton and Moseley were outlying estates of Bromsgrove. Norton means 'north farm'; and the name Northfield may indicate that this place also started life as a northern colony of Bromsgrove.

Another pointer to a dual settlement of the Greater Birmingham area is the fact that, although the majority of its parishes were originally part of the Anglian diocese of Lichfield, Yardley, King's Norton and Northfield belonged to Worcester, a bishopric which is known to have been created in the late seventh century especially to serve the Hwicce people. On the face of it, therefore, the territory covered by this group of parishes looks very much like a tongue of early Saxon penetration into what was otherwise Anglian or Mercian country (see map, page 6).

If, as has been suggested, much of the local landscape remained tree-covered at the end of the Roman period, one of the main problems which faced the English newcomers would have been the finding, or making, of suitable forest clearings, where they could raise their corn and keep their cattle. No doubt this is why so many of the local Anglo-Saxon place-names end in the 'clearing' element-*ley*. We have already met this in Weoley, and it is also found, for instance, in Saltley, Bartley (now Bartley Green), and Selley (now Selly Oak). Originally *lēah* meant 'wood' but it soon came to mean 'clearing or glade in a wood', and this must be the sense implied in most local examples. Such clearings would often have been small at first. We still use the word 'yard' for a small piece of ground, and Yardley probably meant 'small clearing'. So perhaps did Moseley, or 'mouse clearing' which looks like an example of Anglo-Saxon humour — one of the smallest fields in mid-nineteenth-century Yardley bore the name Mouse Park!

Quite often the name of the leader of a group of settlers seems to have become permanently attached to the place he founded. Edgbaston means '*Ecgbeald's* farm', Erdington '*Eored's* farm', Handsworth '*Hūn's* enclosure or homestead'. For all we know, some of the settlements could have been started by individual families. But more often it is likely that small communal groups were involved. This was certainly so at Birmingham, which is actually a group name meaning 'homestead — or meadow — (*ham*) of the people (*ing*) of *Beorma*'.

Wherever it has been possible to work out early settlement points, these appear always to have been associated with open- or common-field land — or in other words, land which during the Middle Ages was divided into long, narrow strips and farmed in common by groups of villagers.

The original settlement site in the manor and parish of Sheldon was not at the village of Sheldon itself, where the parish church came ultimately to be built. Instead it was a mile to the north at Mackadown, which features in the Domesday Book as *Machitone*, meaning '*Macca's* farm'. Macca's name has still not disappeared from the maps. A Mackadown Farm survived into the present century, while Mackadown Lane — which Macca himself probably laid out — continues to serve as an important thoroughfare in the Tile Cross area. When detailed information becomes available for Sheldon manor in the thirteenth century we find that there are three small common fields here, called Elder Field, Rye-eddish Field and Ridding.

The site of Mackadown Farm, and probably of the original Machitone settlement. The late surviving prefab — themselves about to pass into history — seem somehow appropriate.

It is not difficult to believe that this spot would have been attractive to Macca. Whereas the rest of Sheldon is almost entirely covered by Keuper Marl, at Mackadown we find two isolated patches of glacial sand. Obviously, this lighter soil would have been much easier to clear and cultivate than the densely forested clay. Other Saxon pioneers were equally careful in picking their settlement sites. An almost identical situation was chosen at Yardley, where the original open fields on their small sand patch were located immediately north of the medieval church and village (see map, page 19).

These marl lands of Sheldon and Yardley, and the rest of eastern Birmingham, represent the north-western fringe of the ancient Forest of Arden, which stretched across most of north Warwickshire, from the Tame to the Avon valley. On the west, however, they are brought to an abrupt end by the 14 mile long ridge of Keuper Sandstone, which runs diagonally across Greater Birmingham, from Sutton to Northfield.

Beyond this ridge the bedrock is provided by Bunter Sandstone and Bunter Pebble Beds, which are in turn overlain by extensive stretches of glacial drift. The infertile nature of the Bunter Pebble, and the heath-wood landscape it tends to

Sheldon — Medieval Topography.

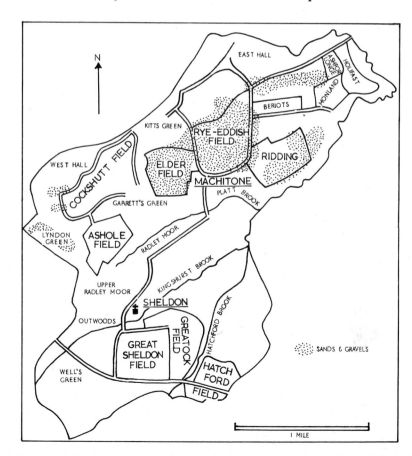

support, can be well seen in Sutton Park. Confronted with a barren terrain of this kind, the best settlement points were to be found at its edges. It is little wonder, then, that the long, narrow sandstone ridge seems to have attracted Anglo-Saxon settlers almost like a fly-paper. In 1086 no less than nine Domesday manors lie astride it: Sutton, Erdington, Aston, Birmingham, Edgbaston, Selly, Northfield, Tessall and Rednal.

From the above, it follows that we can best think of the Greater Birmingham area in Domesday times as falling into three parts: the eastern marl lands or Arden fringe, the western Bunter lands, and — forming both a divide and bridge between them — the ridge of Keuper Sandstone.

Domesday Book records six settlements on the Arden fringe: Minworth, Machitone, Yardley, Moseley, (King's) Norton and Lindsworth. The whole Forest of Arden was extremely thinly populated at this time; and north Arden averaged only 4 recorded adults per square mile in Domesday Book, compared with 11 per square mile for the Feldon district of south-east Warwickshire. Our own manors could not even match the north Arden average. Precise details are lacking for Moseley, King's Norton and Lindsworth, but Sheldon and Yardley taken together produce an estimated population density of only about 1.6 recorded adults — or heads of households — per square mile. Most of the area was still thickly forested. Indeed, on the basis of the Domesday information, it is reckoned that Sheldon and Yardley had at least 7½ square miles of woodland out of a total area of just over 14 square miles. By contrast, there was only enough cleared arable land to employ about 10 plough teams, which is unlikely to have represented more than 1,200 acres. The potential of these marl manors was considerable. But little had yet been done to realize it.

Geographers classify the Bunter lands of west Birmingham as part of the South Staffordshire Uplands, where the average Domesday population was 3 recorded adults per square mile. Handsworth, in which there were two Domesday holdings, plentiful water meadows and two mills along the River Tame, was one of Birmingham's more prosperous manors, with a value of £5. (Domesday valuations are believed to have been rough estimates of the annual rent at which an estate could be leased, complete with its existing stock.) Apart from Handsworth, however, the Bunter lands were as thinly populated as the Arden fringe. Harborne, Perry (Barr) and Witton were all small vills valued at a mere £1.

Turning finally to the Keuper Sandstone settlements, since the ridge is never much above a mile across and frequently less, several of the manors which were strung along it included tracts

The Domesday Manors of Grea[t] Birmingham. Figures give the va[lue] of manors in 1086.

16

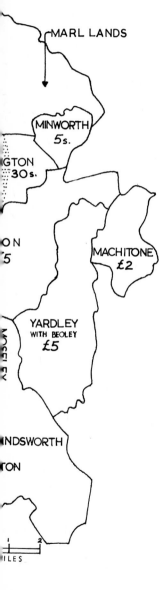

STONE RIDGE

MARL LANDS

MINWORTH
5s.

GTON
30s.

ON
5

MACHITONE
£2

YARDLEY
WITH BEOLEY
£5

NDSWORTH

TON

MILES

of both Bunter and Keuper marl land, as well as small areas of light drift soil. Northfield, which was sited on a narrow neck of glacial drift, with the Rea on one side and Merritts Brook on the other, had been worth as much as £8 in 1066, though twenty years later its value was down to £5. Fourteen plough teams were at work here, suggesting about 1,700 acres of arable land. This in turn implies that some of the fertile marl which this manor possessed must already have been cleared and brought into cultivation. Thirty-three adults were recorded. If one allows four dependents for everyone likely to have had a family, this gives an estimated population total of about 154.

Although Sutton and Aston had much more land to the east of the ridge than Northfield, a great deal of this must have remained untouched. As compared with Northfield's estimated 180 acres of woodland, in the huge manor of Sutton there was an estimated 2,880 acres, in Aston 2,160 acres. Nevertheless, like Northfield, both these vills were relatively well developed. Sutton is recorded as having possessed enough arable land to employ 22 ploughs, though − for some reason − only 8 plough teams were at work at the time of the survey. Sutton's adult population consisted of 20 villeins (villagers), 4 smallholders and 2 slaves. At Aston, with 18 plough teams, there was probably over 2,000 acres of cultivated arable land. Moreover, its 45 recorded adults point to a total population of about 220, which was the highest in the district.

The manor of Birmingham, situated roughly at the centre of the ridge, and overlooking the River Rea, presents a very different picture from the big tripartite manors. For the Rea was Birmingham's eastern boundary, which meant that it was completely excluded from the potentially rich marl lands beyond. 'We know of nothing . . . except sand and gravel', wrote Hutton. That on the ridge itself was reasonably fertile. But the rest, much of it unadulterated Bunter Pebble, was even in the eighteenth century, 'a shameful waste'. When these limitations are borne in mind, together with the manor's relatively small size, Birmingham's poor showing in the Domesday Book is perhaps understandable. The future metropolis of the midlands had only 10 recorded adults and, like three of the four exclusively Bunter-based manors, was valued at £1. In 1086, then, it was one of the poorest manors in one of the poorest parts of central England.

The Great Expansion

Nationally, the eight or nine generations which followed the Norman Conquest brought a tremendous increase in numbers. In fact, the population of England and Wales went up from about 1,500,000 in 1086 to at least 4,000,000 by 1300, and perhaps to as much as 6,000,000. Such growth would simply not have been possible without a corresponding increase in food production; and this in turn meant that a great deal of new land had to be brought under cultivation. But since backward areas like our own still had many thousands of acres of uncultivated waste and woodland, throughout the twelfth and thirteenth centuries local populations were able to increase steadily. All over the Greater Birmingham district, therefore, around the little settlements of Saxon date, new hamlets and also isolated farmsteads were soon being founded, and countless new fields carved out of the waste to support them.

In the manor of Yardley new hamlets appeared at Tenchlee (later known as Acock's Green), Lee (now Lea Village) and Greet. Like the parent settlement, all three were situated on or near stretches of light, easily worked soil — the name Greet actually means 'gravel'. Like Yardley, too, each new hamlet had

The barn of Pinfold House, with the gable end of the timber-framed, but Georgianized, farmstead beyond. This is the only remaining pointer to the dispersed hamlet of Tenchlee or Acock's Green.

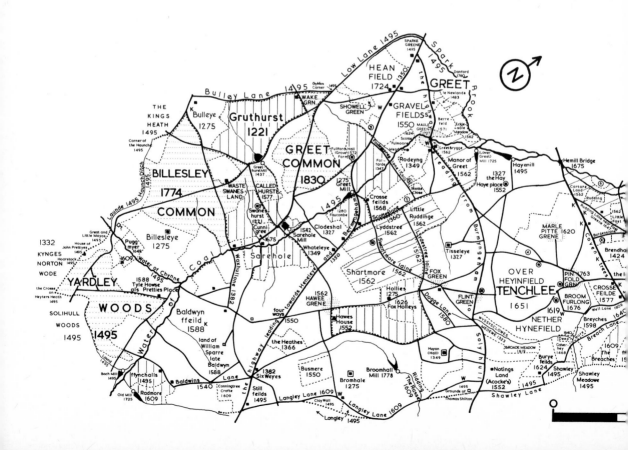

its own set of common fields. This suggests that, as in Saxon times, the land must have been cleared by small groups of people, working together.

But not all Arden peasants favoured co-operative enterprise. Some went off into the forest and, over a period of years, or perhaps over several generations, they and their families laboriously cleared thirty or forty acres of their own. People like this did not have to farm in common with others. They made banks and hedges to enclose their private clearings, or 'assarts'; and built their farmsteads, not in the communal hamlet, but amidst their own fields. Eventually, too, the owners of many of these outlying farms dug a moat round their farmstead – to deter marauding men and animals, to stock with fish, and perhaps also to show off to their neighbours. Eleven certain, and three other possible moats are on record for Yardley.

As before, a place-name often immortalized the 'developer'. The man who first opened up Tyseley was known as *Tyssa* – the name meaning *'Tyssa's* clearing'. Similarly, Billesley means *'Bill's* clearing'. Down to the seventeenth century Hall Green was not Hall Green at all, but *Haw* Green; and this was because the Haw family had carved out a farm for themselves in that area, the farm being known as Haw House – and later Hall Green Hall.

YARDLEY – MEDIEVAL TOPOGRAPHY

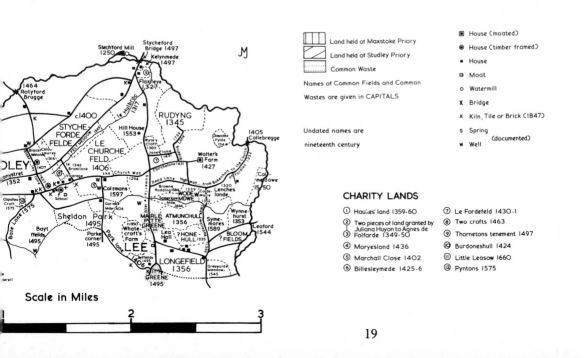

▦	House (moated)
◉	House (timber framed)
▪	House
◘	Moat
o	Watermill
X	Bridge
k	Kiln, Tile or Brick (1847)
s	Spring (documented)
w	Well

Land held of Maxstoke Priory
Land held of Studley Priory
Common Waste

Names of Common Fields and Common Wastes are given in CAPITALS

Undated names are nineteenth century

CHARITY LANDS

① Haukes' land 1359-60
② Two pieces of land granted by Juliana Huyon to Agnes de Folfarde 1349-50
④ Moryeslond 1436
⑤ Marchall Close 1402
⑥ Billesleymede 1425-6
⑦ Le Fordefeld 1430-1
⑧ Two crofts 1463
⑨ Thornetons tenement 1497
⊗ Burdoneshull 1424
⑪ Little Leasow 1660
⑫ Pyntons 1575

Scale in Miles

Other private clearances were made at Swanshurst, Sarehole, Shaftmoor, Broomhall, Gilbertstone, Hay Hall and Blakesley. Every one of these names is still to be found on the map of Birmingham, while at Hay Hall and Blakesley ancient farmsteads survive.

Not all the appropriated land was devoted to agricultural purposes. By 1300 Yardley, Aston, Handsworth, and indeed most other local manors, had their hunting parks — that is to say, areas of heath and woodland that were enclosed and preserved in their natural state in order to provide pleasure and venison for their manorial lords. Locally, the largest and finest of these medieval game reserves was the 2,500 acre Sutton Park, which was established in 1125 by the then Earl of Warwick, and which today provides such a remarkable oasis of wildlife within 6 miles of the city centre.

By the early thirteenth century so much private clearance and enclosure had taken place that the main body of peasants tried to call a halt to it. For the community at large was becoming dangerously short of common waste or pasture, which was vital to small farmers for the grazing of their cattle. In 1221 Thomas Swanshurst of Yardley had his recently planted hedges pulled down by 19 of his neighbours; and in the same year other angry peasants threw down a bank of Richard son of Edwin, and a hedge of Walter son of Richard.

It was during this period that the feet of the local peasants trod out the intricate communications network of Yardley manor. These unmade tracks were not planned in any modern sense; they evolved by use and wont, becoming fixed only if they answered to the long-term needs of the peasantry. Yet, just as the place-names of the early medieval period still provide the basic nomenclature of the area, so most of its routeways have remained in use to the present day.

By 1275 the population of Yardley had risen to about 800 and the whole of the manor had been brought under cultivation; except, that is, for the precious stretches of common pasture — like Yardley Wood and Swanshurst Common — which the lesser peasantry had fought so hard to preserve.

In the smaller Arden parish of Sheldon there was a much higher proportion of communal clearance than at Yardley; and this in turn produced a considerably higher proportion of common-field land, as against privately cleared enclosures. Furthermore, here the new colony village of Sheldon eventually surpassed its parent Machitone in importance. This was probably because Sheldon was based on clay, which once it had been cleared of forest would prove more fertile than the sand of Machitone.

Details are lacking for the parishes and manors situated on the Bunter lands to the west of Birmingham. Good soil was harder to find here; but it is safe to assume that every acre available would have been brought into cultivation at this time. The same would apply to the parishes athwart the sandstone ridge. Down to 1086 we know of only three communal settlements in the parish of Aston: Aston itself, Witton and Erdington. By 1300 a further seven are on record: Bordesley, Duddeston, Nechells, Saltley, Little Bromwich, Castle Bromwich and Water Orton. In view of the Domesday manor of Aston's extensive arable acreage, several of these may well have been pre-Conquest developments. But others were no doubt founded in the two-thousand acres of Domesday woodland during the twelfth and thirteenth centuries.

By 1300, then, most of the Greater Birmingham area had been cleared of natural woodland; most of its villages, hamlets and isolated farmsteads had been founded and named; and most of its ancient roads and trackways established.

The character of our ancient parish churches is another legacy of the Great Expansion. Little or nothing remains of the early medieval church fabrics at Sutton, Aston, Edgbaston, Handsworth or Harborne. But elsewhere, apart from towers and spires, which are generally of fifteenth-century date (see page 33), most of the surviving medieval work belongs to the thirteenth or early fourteenth centuries. Indeed, so much church building and rebuilding took place in local parishes at this time that two round-headed windows at King's Norton and a doorway of c. 1170 at Northfield are all that survives from the preceding Norman period. However, some particularly fine thirteenth-century work can be seen at Northfield, with its 'complete and unspoilt' Early English chancel, while at King's Norton, Yardley and Sheldon the main emphasis is on the Decorated style which was in vogue from about 1290 to 1370.

A Market Centre

Surviving subsidy rolls, or tax returns, show that the manor of Birmingham, having been one of the poorest local settlements in Domesday times, had by the early fourteenth century become the most populous and prosperous place in the whole of the Greater Birmingham area (see page 31).

Yet the growth of Birmingham – unlike that of surrounding communities – cannot have been due to forest clearance and the making of new farms. On the contrary, there was probably less scope for agricultural expansion here than on almost any other nearby estate. For, apart from Birmingham's relatively small size and extensive stretches of infertile soil, the map of the medieval parish shows that the de Birmingham family, its manorial lords, kept a particularly high proportion of territory in their own hands. In the sixteenth century – and probably in the twelfth – virtually all the land east of Smallbrook Street (now Queensway) and Dale End belonged to the lord's private holding or demesne, as did a large hunting ground called Rotton Park in the south-west quarter of the manor. When to this we add the fact that the whole of the north-west quarter was occupied by the sterile waste known as Birmingham Heath, it will be apparent that only about 1,000 out of Birmingham's 3,000 acres could ever have been available for peasant cultivation.

Much ink has been spilled trying to explain the rise of Birmingham. Yet the usual explanations – its proximity to the Black Country, the convergence of routeways on the Deritend ford, and so on, – merely tell us why, having once become the district's main market centre, it subsequently grew and prospered. They do not tell us why this manor, rather than any other, developed as a market town in the first place. And indeed, however strange it may seem, it is not the physical advantages of Birmingham but its physical disadvantages that come closest to explaining this initial take-off. In fact, with little prospect of creating new fields and farmsteads, if Birmingham was not to remain for ever an inconsequential hamlet, it had no alternative but to develop as a place of trade.

The initiative came early: and this no doubt goes a long way towards explaining its success. For in seeking to launch a new market town, being first off the mark in a given area could be an important advantage. It was probably not until the mid twelfth century that the surrounding villages had grown sufficiently to warrant the setting up of a trading centre in their midst. Peter de Birmingham made sure that that centre would be in his own manor. The Earls of Warwick waited until 1300 before obtaining from the Crown a market charter for their township of Sutton.

The Bull Ring Market today. Open markets have been held on this spot for over 800 years.

Right:
The Manor of Birmingham (after Conrad Gill).

Two Birmingham road names that recall demesne holdings in the medieval manor.

The grant which Peter purchased between 1154 and 1166, giving him the right to hold a market every Thursday at Birmingham, was not only the earliest market charter for Warwickshire, but for the whole of the Birmingham Plateau. Nor need we assume that Birmingham's commercial career necessarily began at this precise date, still less that it was the manorial lord's idea. Go-ahead or impoverished tenants might well have started supplementing their income by marketing activities some time previously. But whoever was responsible, the important thing was that country people from a wide area around had probably got into the habit of trading at Birmingham long before its immediate rivals – Walsall, Wednesbury, Dudley, Halesowen, Bromsgrove, Solihull, Coleshill or Sutton – had entered into competition.

The market charter was followed by the purchase (in 1250) of the right to hold an annual four day fair at Ascensiontide; and, just as importantly, by the lords of the manor deciding to transform their market village into a manorial borough. For all we know, this latter move could have come quite soon after 1166, but it is not until 1250, when John de Stodley is described as 'burgess of Birmingham', that we get the first clear evidence of borough status.

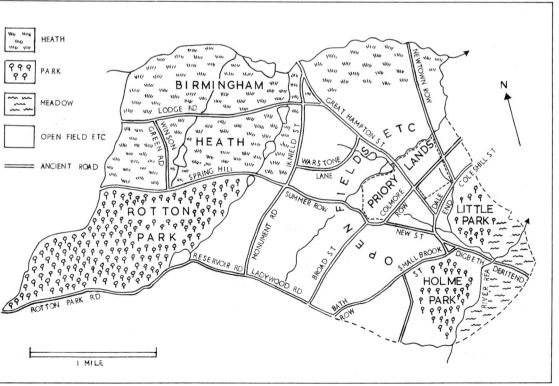

Burgesses were freemen holding a burgage tenement, which consisted of a house plot in the town or 'Borough' itself, and sometimes a few acres in the fields of the 'Foreign'. Among the earliest burgesses would have been native peasants who were encouraged to change or 'commute' the labour services they owed their lord into a money rent. A transaction of 1232, by means of which a number of tradesmen purchased freedom from the hay-lifting services formely due to William de Birmingham, very likely represents the concluding stages of this process. But as well as freeing natives from restrictive feudal practices, burgage tenure also had the advantage of attracting newcomers.

With climbing populations all around, there would be no lack of young men on the look out for such opportunities. A thirteenth century villein who escaped from his native manor and managed to obtain a burgage holding in Birmingham would also escape from the servile status into which he had been born. But it would be a mistake to think of Birmingham as an isolated haven of freedom. Many of the peasants in the surrounding countryside enjoyed free status anyway. At Yardley all those who had gone into the waste and made their own enclosed farms, or assarts, came into this category: and such people may well have accounted for as much as two-thirds of the whole parish community. Moreover, since a freeman, unlike a villein, was at liberty to leave his native manor, the existence of these large free populations throughout the area must have made Birmingham's recruitment drive that much easier.

In the thirteenth and early fourteenth centuries surnames were not yet fully hereditary, and where a person was not a native of the place in which he lived, he was sometimes called after the place from which he came. The earliest recorded burgess presumably haled from Studley in Worcestershire. An analysis of the Lay Subsidy Roll of 1332 suggests that 18 out of 69 taxpayers − or 1 in 4 − were recent arrivals. Some of the lesser place-names cannot now be identified with certainty, but among those which present no difficulty are Norton, Packwood, Hodnell, Coleshill, Hinckley and Bilston.

This influx of newcomers would have involved major topographical changes within the town of Birmingham itself, for new burgage plots had to be laid out to accommodate them. There is not a scrap of documentary evidence which will enable us to discover how this first 'remaking of Birmingham' was accomplished; and most of the field evidence has now disappeared. All we can do is to try to work out a logical sequence of developments, remembering the lie of the land, the evidence from other, better documented boroughs, and making use of such early maps as are available. Even then the result can never be hard historical fact, only plausible conjecture.

The most likely site for the twelfth century village is represented today by the Bull Ring which may well have begun its millenium and more of service to the community as the village green. It was immediately below this that the first little church of St. Martin was erected in Norman times, while close-by Moat Lane still reminds us of the position of the moated de Birmingham manor house.

If we are right in thinking that the homesteads of the early villagers were grouped round the Bull Ring, then it is probable that the first burgage tenements were in this area, as well as along Edgbaston Street, perhaps, and along High Street. Some of them, indeed, may have been the ancient villein house plots, little altered except in name and status. But in the gaps between these existing properties the lord's surveyor may have laid out new burgages, giving them the long, narrow shape which was their hallmark.

The eighteenth century maps of Birmingham clearly depict these strip-like burgage plots; and if they are trustworthy, the borough as so far defined would have provided something like 75 of them. For a time, perhaps, this would have been enough. But

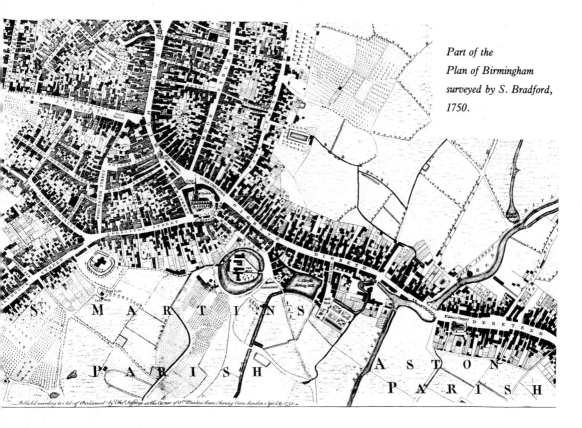

Part of the
Plan of Birmingham
surveyed by S. Bradford,
1750.

25

with the influx of new burgesses, eventually an extension of the borough area would be called for.

When New Street was new we do not know. Originally the land on either side of it probably formed part of Birmingham's common fields, which appear to have stretched in a wide arc round the north and west of the township. However, fifteenth and sixteenth century deeds speak of burgages along Newstrete, while the straightness and generous width of its lower end undoubtedly give it the appearance of being a planned thoroughfare. Possibly, therefore, New Street was laid out, and the open-field ridges or strips — at least to the north of it — converted into burgage plots, at a fairly early date.

But equally early — if not earlier — expansion must also have taken place along either side of Digbeth and Deritend, where the characteristic burgage layout is even more unmistakable. In some ways this eastward extension was far from ideal. For the land in the low-lying Rea valley was unpleasantly damp and watery, and the river itself extremely liable to flood. Yet the advantages which were to be gained by pushing out a long, octopus-like tentacle in this direction far outweighed any physical inconveniences.

Historians divide the many hundreds of new market towns that came into existence during this period of rapid population growth and economic prosperity into two main groups. Firstly, there are the so-called 'organic' boroughs, which are thought to have evolved naturally on the site of an already existing village settlement. By contrast, the term 'planted' borough denotes an entirely new creation — or in other words, a town that was laid out on a virgin site by an ambitious lord.

The usual position for a village — and therefore for an organic borough — was near the centre of its manorial territory, so that peasants could reach all their farmland without travelling too far from the homesteads. Planted boroughs, on the other hand, were often established at the very edge of a rural parish. In particular, a bridge over a river, which was also a parish boundary, was considered an ideal focus for such a place. If burgage plots could be laid out on both sides of the bridge, then the people of two parishes, instead of one, would find themselves caught up in the new venture, automatically using the market, and perhaps being tempted to move house and set up as burgesses.

Assuming that Birmingham's first burgage plots were along the original village streets, then this would make it an organic borough. However, owing to the infertile nature of the western part of the manor, the original settlement was not centrally placed, but well over to the east. This gave its lords the chance of imitating the planters of completely new townships. The chance

Needless Alley. This probably owes its curious shape to the fact that it was once a fordrough between open-field strips. Because of the turning problem of the long medieval plough team, such strips invariably acquired a reversed-S shape, or 'aratral curve'.

Above:
The Old Crown Inn, Deritend. This predominantly early sixteenth-century house is the only ancient building that still stands on a Birmingham burgage plot.

Right:
The Golden Lion, removed from Deritend to Cannon Hill Park in 1911.

Below:
Digbeth and Deritend as shown on Buck's Prospect of Birmingham from the South West, 1731.

was not missed. By plumping for an urban extension along Digbeth, the de Birminghams carried the borough right down to the River Rea, which was then, and for long afterwards, the parish boundary between Birmingham and Aston. By extending their burgage plots beyond the Rea into Deritend they obtained a bridgehead in Aston itself.

Birmingham shared a common overlord with Aston, in the Baron of Dudley. But how precisely its manorial lords engineered this earliest of Birmingham take-overs we do not know. That they did so is beyond question. Medieval pottery recovered from Deritend in 1953, and now displayed in the City Museum, suggests that the new development was well under way by the mid-thirteenth century. Similarly, an encroachment on a road in the 'town of Bermingeham' and the 'parish of Aston' which was reported in 1276 can only refer to Deritend. In any case, when we first hear of *Duryzatehende* by name in 1381 its lord is clearly stated to be Sir John de Birmyneham.

Occasional documentary references to textile, leather and iron workers occur during the thirteenth and early fourteenth centuries. Nevertheless, the town's early success was undoubtedly due more to commercial than to industrial activities. One of the main functions of a medieval market town was to serve as a selling and buying point for local surplus produce. Birmingham clearly had a flourishing cattle market by the mid-thirteenth century: for the bailiffs of Rowington, fifteen miles to the south-east, regularly sent their livestock here, in preference to Stratford and other nearer, geographically more convenient centres. Similarly, the fleeces from local sheep flocks must have found a ready market in Birmingham. John atte Holte and Walter de Cloddeshale, who were among the town's highest taxpayers in the subsidy roll of 1332, are known to have traded in wool. The same tax list also provides a hint of Birmingham's growing role as a local service centre. As well as a mason and two barbers, its occupational surnames include two mercers, who would presumably have specialized in bringing such luxuries as wines, spices, unusual foodstuffs and the more exotic textiles, from distant parts.

Another clue to Birmingham's early importance as a trading centre is provided by the wheel-like pattern of roads which radiate out from it, and most of which are known to have been in existence by 1400. Hutton speaks of twelve roads going out from Birmingham 'which point to as many towns', and describes how they had been 'worn by the long practice of ages into deep holloways, some of them twelve or fourteen yards below the surface of the banks, with which they were once even'.

The basic route pattern was in the form of a double fan. Roads to the north, west and south – i.e., to Lichfield, Stafford, Wolverhampton, Dudley, Halesowen and Worcester – fanned out from the Bull Ring; and so did the road to Coleshill, due east of Birmingham, which crossed the Rea at Duddeston. The other, smaller fan was centred on the eastern end of Deritend and covered the south-east quarter of the compass, with roads to Coventry, Warwick, Stratford and Alcester. Thus there were two nodal points, one to the west of the Rea, the other to the east. Joining them across the valley, like the bar of a dumb-bell, was the long, burgaged street of Digbeth and Deritend, which therefore had to be used by all east-west traffic, except that from Coleshill. There is no reference to a bridge until the later Middle Ages. But, although a natural island divided the river into two arms here, thereby making it relatively easy to ford, it seems unlikely that the de Birminghams – having gone to the expense of 'planting' both sides of the river with burgage plots – would not also have provided a dry means of crossing it.

High Street, Bordesley. The marked difference in level between pavement and road still reminds us that the ancient thoroughfare was once 'holloway'.

Below:
A familiar road name which provides evidence of the same phenomenon.

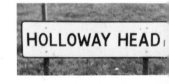

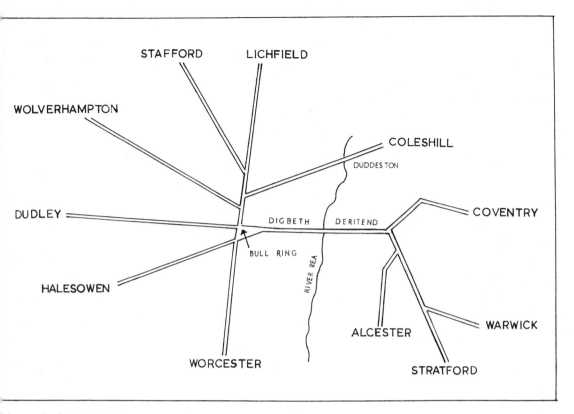

Diagram showing the 'double fan' of medieval roads centred on Birmingham.

The most important west-east road was that from Shrewsbury and Dudley, to Coventry. This was used by the growing Welsh and North of England cattle trade passing through Birmingham for the south. Although Coventry got most of its iron at this time from the Forest of Dean, some Dudley iron may already have been reaching it by the same route. But the road which earned Birmingham a place on the well-known Gough Map of c.1330 was the south-north highway from Worcester and Droitwich, to Lichfield. Following the full length of the sandstone ridge between Northfield and Sutton this served as a saltway and was said to have been one of the 'Four great Royal Roads' of England. By chance, we know that in 1340 a consignment of wine, having been shipped up the River Severn from Bristol, was then transported in carts along this road, to Birmingham.

Most of the other routes would, as yet, have been of only minor significance. More traffic would have come in from Moseley than from Alcester, from Sutton than from Stafford. For Birmingham was far from being the hub of the medieval midlands. The really important places still lay beyond the edge of

29

the Birmingham Plateau: the three county towns of Stafford, Warwick and Worcester, the religious centres of Pershore, Evesham and Lichfield, and above all, of course, Coventry, the region's only major industrial town.

All the same, Birmingham, which had entered the Middle Ages with smaller achievements and bleaker prospects than most of the surrounding manors, had by 1300 completely outstripped them on both counts. The financial outlays which its manorial lords must have made in the buying of royal charters, the laying out of burgage plots, and the attraction of new settlers, were now repaying them handsomely. Not only were they drawing fat profits from the long rent roll of burgesses, but also from the rents of booths and stalls set up in the market place, from the tolls paid by strangers who came to sell their goods here, and from the fines charged for the breaking of market regulations.

During the late thirteenth century, while neighbouring parishes were having to content themselves with adding aisles and transepts to their village churches, the lords and burgesses of Birmingham were able to completely rebuild St. Martin's in the fashionable Decorated style.

It was during this period, too, that Birmingham's first charitable institution, the Hospital, or Priory, of St. Thomas was established. Little is known of the origin, or for that matter the precise purpose, of this thirteenth century foundation. But the extensive lands it came to occupy to the immediate north of the town seem — like the New Street burgage plots — to have been taken out of the common fields. Still further open-field land was probably being enclosed at much the same time, in order to provide local graziers and butchers with pastures on which they could fatten their livestock for market. Do such depredations mean that Birmingham was already so confident of its ability to live by trade that it was turning its back on the growing of corn? In any case, the occurrence of so much early enclosure may go a long way towards explaining why Birmingham's common fields should have disappeared with a haste and completeness which is quite unparalleled amongst its neighbours.

All that remains of 'the Priory' today, apart from the road name 'Priory Queensway' is a fragment of moulded stone rescued by Hutton and now in the City Museum. After at least two rebuildings, little survives of the medieval St. Martin's either. Yet those who penetrate the dark, sepulchre-like Victorian interior may still find the recumbent effigies of three of its thrustful de Birmingham lords.

Stone effigies in St. Martin's Church believed to be of Sir William c Birmingham, c. 1325 (above), and S Fulk de Birmingham, c. 137 (below).

30

The Rural Recession

Nationally the second half of the thirteenth-century represents the high water mark of medieval colonization. Populations then stood at a peak which was not to be reached again for three hundred years; more land was under cultivation than ever before; farming and trade, village and market town were flourishing. But by the end of the century the tempo of growth was beginning to flag. Numbers had advanced to the limits of natural resources as they could at that time be exploited; the land would feed no more people; for many existence was becoming marginal in the extreme. Then from 1312 came a run of bad harvests, culminating in the torrential rains and Great Famine of 1315-17. There was almost universal crop failure; grain prices soared alarmingly; tens of thousands died of starvation.

It would be a fortunate area which passed unscathed through these difficult times; and, if any such existed, it is to be feared that ours was not among them. In Worcestershire the number of settlements appearing on the subsidy rolls declined from 280 in 1275 to 222 in 1327, tax-paying households from 7,373 to 4,644. The 1327 roll for Yardley is known to be unreliable. Because of evasions, as well as exemptions on grounds of poverty, the listed tax-payers may well represent as little as 40% of the total number of households. Even allowing for this, however, it seems likely that Yardley's population, which had been about 800 in 1275, must have dropped to at least 600 by 1327; or in other words, by something like 25% in fifty years.

Alongside this population decline came a serious slump in the economic prosperity of the community. Yardley's taxed wealth had been £164 in 1275; by 1327 it was down to £61. The average taxed estate of those appearing on the earlier roll had been 41 shillings (£2.05); on the later 26 shillings (£1.30). The subsidy rolls for other rural parishes in the Greater Birmingham area suggest an equally gloomy picture. In 1327 Edgbaston had a mere 19 taxpayers who together mustered £1. 4s. 6d. (£1.22½); Erdington had 14 rendering £1. 11s. 3d. (£1.56). Birmingham alone makes a reasonable showing. With 75 householders providing £7. 0s. 6d. (£7.02½) from taxed estates assessed at £140.50 — recession or not — it was now the third most populous and fourth most prosperous place in Warwickshire.

A generation after the Great Famine came the Black Death, which nationally is thought to have reduced numbers by at least a third. There is little direct evidence of its impact locally. But a study of Yardley surnames leaves no doubt that the Great Famine and the bubonic plague together caused a major population upheaval. Between 1300 and 1374 no less than 72 out of 147 established families disappear from the record.

31

From the material point of view, the fifteenth century has a reputation that is not much better than the fourteenth. Still the general background is believed to have been one of struggling populations and widespread stagnation. Yet, according to a recent study, Warwickshire and Worcestershire increased their wealth between 1334 and 1515 at a faster rate than many other counties. Lesser peasants may have found it difficult to eke out a living. At Yardley in the early fifteenth century the rents of some of the smaller holdings had to be reduced, while others fell vacant for want of a tenant. However, the more robust or more fortunate members of the peasantry were able to exploit these conditions to their advantage, gradually acquiring unwanted acres until they had built up really big estates.

Another important development of this period was in land use. With smaller populations, less corn was required; so there was a reduction in the proportion of arable land. In the fifteenth and early sixteenth century the Birmingham area had a mainly pastoral economy. Farmers grew enough corn to feed their own families. For profit they concentrated on the rearing of cattle and beef production. Moreover, since this animal husbandry involved comparatively little work, quite a few took up industrial by-employments. Weavers, tanners and smiths were to be found throughout the district. In Arden parishes coopery – the making of tubs, casks and pails from local oaks — became a trade of some importance, while at Yardley tile-making collects its first documentary references at the beginning of the fifteenth century.

Another result of falling numbers was a change in the social structure of local communities. During the early Middle Ages peasant wealth appears to have been fairly evenly distributed. By the end of the fifteenth century so much land had been concentrated into the hands of relatively few families that there was a wider gap between rich and poor than previously. Every parish had its families of 'gentlemen' and substantial 'yeomen' – like the Acocks, the Dolphins, the Ests and the Greswolds of Yardley – who had become extremely wealthy and influential: in fact, a kind of peasant aristocracy.

The late Middle Ages, like other periods, left its monuments for posterity. Well-to-do peasants were concerned to educate their sons; and timber-framed buildings associated with ancient village schools are still to be seen at King's Norton and Yardley. There was little need to increase church accommodation at this time, but wealthy families often established chantry chapels to provide regular intercession for the souls of the departed. The north aisle of St. Giles's church Sheldon was in origin such a foundation; and the north aisle of St. Edburga's Yardley may

have been built to house one or more of its five late-medieval side chapels. During the fifteenth century virtually all the local parishes found the money to build – or heighten – their church tower, and sometimes to provide it with a spectacular steeple. The tower at Sheldon, and the towers and steeples at Yardley and King's Norton, appear to have been built by the same master mason. Inscriptions on the inside stonework at Sheldon give his name as Henry Ulm, as well as recording that he built this tower in 1461 at a cost of £42.4s.8d. (£42.23). At Sutton, Harborne, Handsworth and Aston, where eighteenth- or nineteenth-century rebuilding swept away the whole – or almost the whole – of the ancient church, these fifteenth-century towers and steeples are the only substantial medieval features to have survived.

Birmingham in the Later Middle Ages

Hundreds of English market towns came to grief during the generations which followed the Black Death, and were not revived in the slack economic conditions of the fifteenth century. Warwickshire possessed about 34 in 1300; by 1500 this number had been halved. And even in some of the survivors the markets and fairs had fallen into abeyance. Indeed, this was true of Sutton Coldfield, which was medieval Birmingham's only rival as an urban centre within the Greater Birmingham area. Leland tells us that Sutton, 'stondynge in a barren soyle', 'fell dayly to decay' during the fifteenth century, until 'the market was clene forsaken'. Yet it is as if Birmingham — despite the fact that it also stood 'in a barren soyle' — was already acquiring that knack which has been one of its foremost characteristics in modern times: the knack of riding through a depression. The information available is meagre. But, as far as we can tell, this was a market town that did not so much as falter throughout the late medieval period.

Some of Birmingham's advantages are not difficult to guess. With extensive pasture farming in its surrounding parishes, the livestock market no doubt continued to prosper. Meanwhile, the rise of a wealthy peasantry ensured a steady demand for luxury products. Mercery in particular seems to have become a lucrative business. For this is the time when families of local mercers like the Colmores, the Smallbrooks and the Sheltons were laying the foundations for their future wealth and prominence. In the mid-fifteenth century the town was even managing to support its own goldsmith.

Two road names that recall Birmingham families which rose to prominence in the fifteenth century. In the early eighteenth century Colmore Row was called New Hall Lane, i.e., after the Colmore's New Hall estate.

Left:
Bishop Vesey (c. 1462-1554) made desperate efforts to revive the fortunes of his native Sutton Coldfield. Apart from securing a charter of incorporation, founding a grammar school and introducing kersey weaving, he built a Town Hall, two bridges and 51 stone houses. Ye Olde Stone House, Maney Hill Road, is one of the five surviving Vesey houses.

St. John's, Deritend, as shown on Westley's East Prospect of 1732. Four years later the church was rebuilt, its successor being demolished in 1947.

Above:
Plaque in the Bull Ring.
Below:
The Old Market Cross. The 'roome over it' was built in 1702, and the structure demolished in 1784.

Another indication of Birmingham's relative prosperity is the extent to which its burgesses — or at any rate some of them — were able to provide rich gifts and endowments for the support of gilds, chantries and charities. The most interesting of these foundations was the Gild of the Holy Cross. Besides maintaining several chantry priests, this institution provided almshouses, together with 'alle other kinde of sustenaunce' for members, or relatives of members, who had fallen upon hard times. It also took responsibility for the upkeep of 'two great bridges of stone', one of which was presumably Deritend Bridge. Unusually for an institution of this kind, however, the Gild of the Holy Cross did not concern itself with education. But this may have been because the keeping of a school was one of the tasks undertaken by the Gild of St. John, which was founded at about the same time (c. 1380) in conjunction with the newly built St. John's Chapel, Deritend. Ironically, at the dissolution of the two gilds in 1547 the St. John's school disappeared without trace, while part of the endowment of the Gild of the Holy Cross was used to establish a new 'King Edward VI' grammar school, with its first schoolhouse in the latter's Gild Hall at the lower end of New Street.

The Tudor Market Town

When the relatively plentiful documentation of the sixteenth century allows us for the first time to form a detailed impression of Birmingham's appearance and character, it is clearly a flourishing place. Leland, who passed through it about 1540, called it 'a good market toune', while Camden describes it a generation later as 'swarming with inhabitants' and having 'an abundance of handsome buildings'.

With the help of surveys of the manor and other contemporary records, it is possible to visualize fairly sharply how Tudor Birmingham operated as a market centre. If one goes into the Bull Ring today, on the unnecessarily ugly concrete bridge which carries the Inner Ring Road over it, a circular plaque can be found, recording the site of 'the Old Market Cross'. Beyond, the land falls away to St. Martin's which, in fact, might have been difficult to catch a glimpse of from this point four or five centuries ago, for blocking the view was a line of butchers' shops known as 'the Shambles'. Originally, market traders must simply have set up temporary booths and stalls here, but later these became converted into permanent timber-framed buildings.

The name 'Bull Ring' first occurs in 1550, and the proximity of butchers' shops is probably no accident. At Hereford there was a seventeenth-century bye-law which obliged butchers to bait all bulls before slaughter in order, it was said, to tenderize the meat. Beyond the Shambles, the road running to the right of St. Martin's was Mercer or Spicer Street, where some of the town's principal mercers still had their houses and shops. To the left of St. Martin's in what is now the top end of Digbeth, lay the Corn Cheaping, or corn market. During the eighteenth-century, in times of scarcity, when corn was dear, the farmers and dealers who assembled here with their samples of grain are said to have needed the protection of special constables.

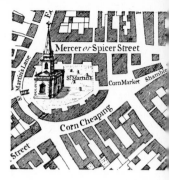

The market area as shown on Westley Plan of 1731.

If we now turn round, the northward view on a Tudor market day would have been filled with 'all maner of bests'. For the whole of High Street served as a cattle market: or rather, as two cattle markets. The English or Rother Market was held in the lower half, and beyond that, the Welsh Market. Several of the 96 borough tenants in 1553 were large graziers who dealt in the English and Welsh markets. So important had the Welsh cattle trade become that the northern part of the town was known as 'Welchend'; and at the top of High Street a 'Welch Cross' was later set up, to partner the Old (English) Market Cross in the Bull Ring. There were also special sales of sheep and cattle at Birmingham's two annual fairs, together with horse sales in Edgbaston Street (transferred to Horse Fair in 1777).

At the junction of High Street with New Street stood the Toll House or 'Tolbooth'. As the name implies, this was where market dues were collected from visiting traders — though not from burgesses — on the cattle and sheep which were sold: 'a penny for three beasts, 4d for twenty, and every hundred sheep 2d'.

The Old Welch Cross, completed in 1706 and demolished in 1803.

The main place for selling dairy produce was where we have been standing, at the top of the Bull Ring. So much so, that in the course of time the Market Cross here, as at Ludlow, came to be called the Butter Cross. Other goods were on offer at the Thursday markets, apart from livestock, corn and other foodstuffs. As early as 1403 Wednesbury men were dealing in linen and woollen cloth, iron, steel and brass.

The markets and fairs brought considerable trade to the town, and were vital for the provisioning of its largely non-food-growing population. All the same, by Tudor times, trade was an accompaniment, rather than the main cause, of its ever growing success. Whatever had been the case before, Birmingham was now flourishing because of its vigour, not only as a marketing, but as a manufacturing centre.

Cloth and Chaffer

The two most prominent early industries grew naturally out of the pastoral economy of the area. The manufacture of wool into cloth seems to have been practised as a specialist occupation at least from the thirteenth century. Four possible Birmingham weavers are mentioned in a document of 1232, while others are occasionally found, both here and in the surrounding villages, at various times thereafter. Craftsmen engaged in the finishing processes – fullers, dyers and shearmen – are also sometimes mentioned.

More significantly, we know that in 1358 a fulling mill was built in a bend of the River Tame at Holford, within the grounds of what is today the ICI works, Witton. By the fifteenth century there was another fulling mill, called a 'Walkmyln', at Erdington; and by the sixteenth, three more were at work near the town of Birmingham itself. Such mills represent the adaptation of water power to fulling – the only process to be mechanized in the textile industry during the medieval period – by means of which great wooden hammers were used to 'walk' and, in so doing, thicken the cloth. Their presence strongly suggests that textile workers must have existed in considerable numbers, even if tantalizingly few are to be found in documents.

The foremost cloth marketing centre in Warwickshire was Coventry, but Birmingham may have been runner-up, albeit a rather poor one. In 1397-8 over 3,000 broadcloths are recorded as having been offered for sale at the former place. The whole of the rest of Warwickshire accounted for about another 150, of which Birmingham handled 44.

Among the clothworkers of Birmingham in the mid sixteenth century was John Elliott, who although described as a 'fuller', was in fact engaged in most of the processes associated with textile manufacture. His property at death included 3 spinning wheels, 4 looms, 5 pairs of shears and 'certain other stuff for a shearman's occupation', as well as a 'drying ground'.

Like textile manufacture, the leather industry was an outgrowth of the district's pastoral economy. Animal skins would have been readily available, while the trees of Arden provided that other essential raw material, oak bark.

A John le Wyte, 'Tannor', is mentioned at Yardley in 1345; and Birmingham itself produces chance references to a tanner, a skinner, a 'corbesserer' and a saddler during the fifteenth century. By early Tudor times, the Birmingham industry was sufficiently well established to attract several leather workers from Alcester and Stratford. Over a dozen tanneries were concentrated along Tanner's Row, a short street just west of the Rea bridge, and in the lower part of Digbeth, where the river and its branch streams provided ample water for the cleaning and steeping of hides. One sixteenth-century tanner, Ralph A'Lees, left at his death goods valued at £100, including 80 hides, 450 calf skins and a quantity of bark.

From the early seventeenth century, as a result of a law of James I, two Leather Sealers were appointed annually by the Court Leet for the purpose of inspecting the tanned leather or 'chaffer'. This procedure took place in the Toll House, which consequently later became known as the Leather Hall. Part of the proclamation made by the Crier of the Court Leet when it held its meetings required the public to give information of any tanners 'that sell not good chaffer as they ought', or 'bye the skynnes in any other place than in towne or market'.

Clearly, Birmingham's main leather craft was the primary process of tanning. But saddlery was also practised, by the prominent Elson family among others. With its demand for metal parts, this may have provided a link with what was to become Birmingham's foremost sixteenth- and seventeenth-century industry.

Old smithy and open forge in Digbeth demolished in the early nineteenth century.

The Noise of Anvils

When the sixteenth-century travellers Leland and Camden passed through the 'pretty street' of Deritend, and along Digbeth, 'the beauty of Birmingham', it was not the reek of tanyards which struck them, but 'the noise of Anvils'. Camden speaks of Birmingham's 'great numbers of Smiths', while Leland, in a classic passage, tells us:

> There be many smiths in the towne that use to make knives and all mannour of cutting tooles, and many lorimers that make bites, and a great many naylors. Soe that a great part of the towne is maintained by smithes, who have their iron and sea-cole out of Staffordshire.

Down to this point we have been charting the origin and growth of a very ordinary little market town, and watched it serving and quietly profiting from its own very ordinary hinterland. It would be attributing too much to human foresight, not to mention twelfth-century know-how, to suppose that the de Birminghams, when deciding to establish their manorial borough, took into account the proximity and potential of the

South Staffordshire coalfield. Yet, however unregarded at the start, the extensive coal measures which were to be found beyond the Bunter Pebble Beds, five miles or so to the west of Birmingham, were to prove of overriding importance from the sixteenth century onwards. It was the rise of the Staffordshire iron industry that began to set Birmingham apart from the average run of urban centres, and presaged the rise of the modern industrial giant.

Iron and coal were being extracted at Sedgley and Walsall as early as the thirteenth-century; in 1281 there was a coal mine, an iron mine and 'two Great Forges' at Dudley. But the quantity of iron smelted remained tiny throughout the Middle Ages; and both in the mining district and in the Birmingham area references to specialized metal craftsmen, as opposed to general-purpose smiths, are rare.

However, the early Tudor period brought an expansion of iron production, and since the timber needed for the smelting process was already becoming scarce in the 'Black Country' itself, the industry began to spread into new areas. For apparently, it was easier to carry ironstone to the wood or charcoal, rather than the other way round. Towards the end of the sixteenth century this dispersion of the industry was further encouraged by the development of a new two-stage technology for producing wrought iron, based on the blast furnace and the finery forge, instead of the primitive medieval bloomery. Blast furnaces required water power to drive their bellows; and so did finery forges, with their great water-raised tilt hammers. Furthermore, since the re-capitalized industry operated on a much bigger scale than before, ever greater quantities of charcoal were needed.

The Tame valley, immediately to the north of Birmingham, was able to offer both water and timber. Already in 1538 a bloomery was exploiting the woods of Perry manor, and a decade later we hear of a 'hammer mill' at Handsworth. A new 'furnace for melting and casting iron' was under construction on the Hol Brook at Perry Barr in 1591 when a labourer was killed by falling earth. By 1615 there was a second on the Hockley Brook at Aston. Hutton's description of the 'enormous mountain' of cinder that had accumulated here by his time makes one think of the innumerable wagon trains of Wednesbury iron ore and Arden charcoal that must have passed down the still partially existing Furnace Lane; and of the innumerable cartloads of pig iron that must have gone in the reverse direction.

Blast furnaces could be established on comparatively small watercourses. But forges, where the pig iron was refined by hammering into wrought or bar iron, required a particularly strong head of water and were therefore usually sited on the main stream. Perry Forge was in operation by the 1590s when the names of hammermen, finers and a 'clerk of the forge' occur in the Handsworth parish register. The fulling mill at Holford was converted into a finery forge some time before 1591; by 1605 there was another at Bromford, Castle Bromwich.

The fact that 'smiths', 'lorimers' and 'naylors' were so firmly entrenched in Birmingham when Leland visited the town shows that its metallurgical take-off pre-dated the movement of primary iron production into the Tame valley. Indeed, despite the paucity of documentation, the odds are that this belongs to the fifteenth, rather than to the sixteenth, century. Specialist iron-workers were also at work in the surrounding parishes during the early and mid Tudor period. A lorimer and a lock-smith are found at Handsworth in 1559 and 1561 respectively, while in the latter year four blade mills were working in the same parish. Similarly, several scythesmiths occur at Bordesley, a scythesmith, two wiredrawers and a fletcher (arrow-smith) at Yardley − all before 1540.

It may be misleading to over-emphasize the contribution made by Tame valley iron even in the seventeenth century. Nail-making, cutlery, wire-drawing, etc., all required, not bar, but rod iron. Originally this last was made from bar iron by a laborious manual process, but from the 1620s water-driven rolling and slitting mills were being introduced into the Black Country which did the job mechanically. However, such mills are not found in the Birmingham area until the early eighteenth century: which presumably means that until that time the basic working material of many Birmingham craftsmen had to come from further afield anyway.

Of no less significance than the 'Migration of the Iron Industry' in explaining the rapid growth of metal working during the late sixteenth and early seventeenth centuries may have been the general economic situation in the Birmingham area − and for that matter, the rest of the country − at that time. This had the effect of providing two underlying prerequisites for industrial advance: namely, a growing supply of cheap labour, and a growing demand for consumer products.

Despite extensive redevelopment, the rear of nineteenth-century engineering workshops still marks the line of the old Furnace Lane, Aston (off Porchester Street).

Five Arden Parishes

After the demographic trough of the later Middle Ages, the sixteenth century saw England's population climbing sharply, until by 1600 it was in the region of five million. The last time numbers had approached this dizzy height, there had been an appalling population crisis, culminating in the Great Famine and the Black Death. With renewed population growth, a big problem which confronted England in the first half of the seventeenth century was whether it would be able to break through the crucial five-million barrier at its second attempt; or whether, for a second time, there would be widespread dearth and starvation. In a detailed study of five Arden parishes on Birmingham's eastern periphery (Yardley, Sheldon, Elmdon, Bickenhill and Solihull) over the period 1570-1674 an attempt has been made to look at this problem in so far as our own area is concerned.

In the mid sixteenth-century these parishes still had a pastoral economy, the main emphasis being on the rearing of livestock and meat production. Full-time industrial workers were uncommon, but there was quite a number of farmer and smallholder craftsmen engaged in the textile, leather and wood crafts, as well as some tile-making and metal work.

About 1570 the combined population of the five communities was around the 2,100 mark. But immigration was particularly high over the next 40 years; and this, together with a relatively high local birth rate and low death rate, led to sharply rising numbers. In other parts of the country large areas may have reverted to waste during the late medieval contraction, but here any abandoned land had been promptly added to the farms of the richer, more ambitious peasantry. As a result, the majority of sixteenth-century newcomers had no alternative but to become landless cottagers. This meant in turn that they found themselves faced by two serious difficulties. On the one hand, because local farmers were producing little but beef, it was difficult for them to obtain cheap food. On the other hand, there was a serious shortage of employment.

Over the three generations which span the period 1575-1649, however, local peasants gradually adjusted their farming practice to the new situation. Many ancient pastures were ploughed up for use as temporary arable, the additional acres being sown mainly with the cheap spring grains, barley and oats. At the same time, the pasture itself was used less for the rearing of beef cattle, more for dairying and cheese production.

Together, these agricultural changes began to provide the landless cottagers with a basic bread and cheese diet. They would not have been able to afford even this without employment. Yet, in this respect also, economic and social forces were helping, slowly and painfully, to improve their lot. The swing from pasture to arable itself increased the amount of farm work. For corn-growing and dairying are much more labour intensive than meat production. And, however unexpectedly, another thing that helped eventually to create more jobs was the Tudor price rise. The pressure of population on resources caused food prices to go up by something like 300% over the three generations in question. Obviously this made the problem of keeping body and soul together even more desperate for the poor in the short term. But the concentration of sudden and unaccustomed wealth in the hands of the fortunate, food-producing peasantry also generated a sustained demand for industrial products.

A good deal of the excess agricultural profits was spent on house improvement and the building of new farmsteads. In the mid sixteenth-century the average peasant house was single-storied and contained two or three rooms. By the mid seventeenth century most peasants enjoyed two-storied accommodation, and the average house size had increased to six or seven rooms. Blakesley Hall at Yardley and Stratford Place at Bordesley are surviving examples of the fine houses which were being built by prosperous local yeomen at this time.

Moreover, accompanying this 'Great Rebuilding' came a 'Great Refurnishing'. Peasant halls, which had once contained nothing but a few pieces of rough-hewn furniture, now displayed joined benches, joined tables and turned chairs; kitchens were re-equipped with new wrought iron hearth furniture, brass pots and pans; cupboards became loaded with pewter tableware; the chests in the master's bedroom with flaxen sheets and table linen; the clothes presses with costly raiment.

But someone had to build the new houses, make the new hearth equipment, weave the wool and linen. The late sixteenth-century brought an expansion of brick-making and tile-making at Yardley. In the early years of the seventeenth century we come across a bricklayer for the first time, as well as a thatcher and two tilers. Among woodworkers, the traditional carpenters and coopers are now supplemented by sawyers, joiners, turners and wheelwrights. Weavers become increasingly common. And since it took several pairs of hands to keep one weaver supplied with yarn, carding and spinning are soon being practised in virtually every cottage as a domestic by-employment. Above all, as time goes on, we hear of more and more metal workers.

Many of the landless craftsmen must have been desperately poor. At the age of 38, Humphrey Hodgetts, a nailer of Shirley, 'was not able to get above 4 shillings (20p.) a week' on which to maintain a wife and five children. John Rawlings, a Yardley

weaver, when he died in 1614, had no land, no livestock — only apparel, bed and bedding, and a few household goods. At a time when the average local estate at death was valued at £59, his effects came to a mere £5. 4s. (£5.20).

John Rawlings, indeed, could well have been a victim of the serious population crisis which hit the Five Parishes in the 1610s. Over the 1570-1649 period as a whole, the annual total of baptisms averaged about 20% more than burials. But during the years 1613-17 we find burials exceeding baptisms by over 5%. Although this is not a time of national dearth, or of bad seasons, many of the local poor in these years seem to have been suffering from serious malnutrition, if not dying of starvation.

Nevertheless, this five year local crisis was nothing like the Great Famine or the Black Death. And in fact, England did succeed this time in breaking through the five million barrier. By 1650 its population had risen to almost six million, a figure which was successfully held for three generations, until the unprecedented population rise of the eighteenth and nineteenth centuries, which we associate with the Industrial Revolution.

If our sample is any guide, too, it would seem that even the rural parishes of the Birmingham area made more than their fair contribution. In the 1640s the Five Parishes were managing to support about 3,400 people, which represents over a 50% increase on the 1570 figure.

Men of Iron

From the early sixteenth century two main types of iron worker can be distinguished. Firstly, there were the farmer or smallholder craftsmen, who practised their trade as a by-employment, alongside predominantly pastoral farming. In general these people were independent operators, obtaining their own raw materials, making and marketing their own product. Such a man was the Yardley scythesmith, Edmund Underhill, who died in 1538. Appended to his will is a list of money due to him 'for sythes'. A King's Norton man owed him 27s. (£1.35). In Deritend and Birmingham he had four debtors, with £5.46 outstanding between them. Other customers lived as far afield as Fillongley, Hill Morton (near Rugby) and Bridgnorth.

The second type of worker, landless craftsmen, may have been comparatively rare in Leland's time, except at Birmingham itself. But, for reasons which have already been discussed, they gradually became more widespread, until by the mid-Stuart period they must have provided all but a small proportion of the manpower engaged in the local industry.

The taking up of an iron trade was no doubt encouraged by the relatively small capital outlay involved. The 'one payre of bellows and other naylors tools' left by Robert Harrison of Sheldon in 1645 were valued at £1 − only a third as much as Rawlings's looms. Symon Rotton, a cutler of Yardley, who died in 1634, had £2.15 out of a total estate of £9.40 tied up in industrial equipment, including 'one paire of bellows, one handfeld (anvil), one glasier, one Cutlers sawe, one iron grate, one fyle and one draweing knyffe'.

Dauentny

As time went on, small domestic craftsmen were increasingly organized by ironmongers, or ironmasters, who both supplied their raw materials and marketed the finished articles. In fact, once the ironmongering system had become established, the nailer, wiredrawer or cutler, although working in his own shop at his own anvil, was in effect a wage earner on piece rate.

By rationalizing the supply of iron, and no doubt paying the meanest rate possible for labour, the ironmonger greatly improved the efficiency of the industry. Just as importantly, although at first local markets would have been paramount, the very scale of the bigger ironmongers' operations soon compelled them to look further afield than Fillongley, Hill Morton and Bridgnorth. It was due to their enterprise and business acumen that before the end of the seventeenth century the 'iron and steel wares' of 'Bromichan' were finding 'good vent at London, Ireland and other parts'. Increasingly, too, with the progressive exhaustion of local charcoal supplies − it was reported in the late seventeenth century that many Black Country ironworks were 'decayed for want of timber' – ironmongers had to organize the provision of pig and bar iron from elsewhere. In 1677 Andrew Yarranton explains that 'the greatest part of the Forest of Dean sow iron is sent up the Severn...' and 'at Stourbridge, Dudley, Wolverhampton, Sedgley, Walsall and Birmingham bent, wrought, manufactured into small commodities and diffused all England over, and... into most parts of the world'.

Often ironmongers specialized in a particular branch of the trade, in which case they might be called by a more specific name. Those organizing the manufacture and marketing of nails, for instance, were generally known as nailmasters. Sometimes, too, specialist entrepreneurs actually involved themselves in the manufacturing process. This was particularly common in Birmingham's own foremost specialism, the making of 'all mannour of cutting tooles'. For here, although the early stages of production were farmed out on a domestic basis, the sharpening process took place in blade mills; and these were normally run by ironmonger type figures, even though they might be called cutlers or scythesmiths.

Prince Rupert and 'Birmingham Flames' – from a woodcut in an old Civil War tract, 1643.

Brimidgham

By the mid seventeenth century, Birmingham's dominant edge tool business was sword-making. According to tradition, a Robert Porter who had a blade mill on the River Rea supplied the Parliamentary forces with fifteen thousand swords: an indiscretion which was punished by Prince Rupert in 1643, when, after a skirmish at Camp Hill, he destroyed the offending manufactory, as well as ransacking much of the town.

But the ironmongering family which perhaps did more than any other to spread the fame of Birmingham in the seventeenth-century was the Jennens family. As early as 1625 John Jennens was selling his 'iron ornaments' in the metropolis, through his brother and partner, Ambrose. Later the family seems to have developed its own integrated system of iron production, based on the possession of Aston Furnace and Bromford Forge. Meanwhile, the selling side of the business in London was built up to a point where it involved capital amounting to several thousand pounds. John Jennens commemorated his success by building 'a handsome residence' in High Street, which must have been the biggest house in Birmingham at that time, for in 1663 it heads the Hearth Tax with no less than 25 hearths. It is thought that the family probably began buying up country estates in order to secure charcoal supplies. But whether this was the motive or not, by 1700 John's son, Humphrey, was numbered among the principal landowners in Warwickshire.

Other, lesser dynasties of ironmongers were to be found in the rural villages. The early seventeenth-century inventory of

William Byssell, a Yardley ironmonger-farmer, lists 'iron warre and coffres to laye it in, shoppe tooles, weightes, beame and schales'. As with the Jennens family, the trade was handed on from father to son. A century later (c. 1730) it was reported of George Bissell, 'that he often uses his own team . . . in fetching iron from Birmingham and in carrying of iron goods to several places for sale and uses the same team in husbandry as much as he does in trade'.

Even this rural entrepreneur, it will be noted, obtained his iron supplies through Birmingham. No wonder that Digbeth is reported in 1692 to have 'become a holloway, very dangerous and much out of repair', 'by reason of the daily passing of great numbers of waggons, carts and other carriages, loaded with coals, ironwares and other ponderous goods'.

No wonder either that Birmingham's population was growing. On the best available estimates, it is unlikely to have been more than 1,500 in the mid sixteenth-century; by 1650 it was probably around 5,000. Between 1570 and 1650 the five Arden parishes had managed to cope with roughly a 50% population increase. Birmingham's growth over the same period must have been in the order of 300%. Iron-working was probably practised in something like one in every six households. The 1683 Hearth Tax lists 202 Birmingham properties with smith's hearths, of which 92, or almost half, were in Digbeth and Deritend. The outlying villages could not compete with this degree of concentration. Bordesley had 20 smiths' hearths, Erdington 15, Castle Bromwich 13, Little Bromwich 6.

By the eighteenth century, Birmin‐
ham was producing its own rod iro‐
Westley's Plan of 1731 shows Sampso‐
Lloyd's Slitting & Corn Mills. T‐
street name Mill Lane still points‐
the site of this mill, often referred to‐
the Town Mill.

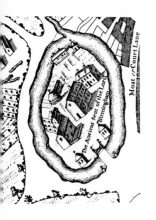

Although changing rapidly, early eighteenth-century Birmingham still had about it many traces of its medieval past: among them the moated de Birmingham manor house — reproduced here from Westley's Plan.

Westley's Birmingham

One of the fascinating things about Birmingham from the historical point of view is the way in which many of the traits that have characterized it in recent times, and which we therefore tend to think of as being of modern origin, turn out in fact to have been recurring themes, leitmotives that were first announced at a much earlier period. The initiative of the Brummie, his willingness to 'chance his arm', and his determination to 'make a go of it' are all epitomized, as it were, in the bold twelfth-century bid to establish a market town long before any potential rivals had entered the field. Birmingham's tradition of attracting immigrants goes back about as far. So does the converse, and yet complementary trait, its shortage of *leibensraum*, and the habit of making room for itself by appropriating other people's territory. In a sense, the making of Greater Birmingham began with the pinching of Deritend from Aston, way back in the thirteenth century. Even Birmingham's indubitable 'luck' seems to have been around from the beginning: in the fact, for instance, that it just *happened* to be sited at the point which ultimately turned out to be 'the natural gateway of the South Staffordshire coalfield'. Yet another characteristic trait is Birmingham's habit of transforming itself. Natives who return today after fifteen or twenty years absence simply do not recognize the place. Mid-Victorian repatriots went through the same experience. And even they were not the first. An inhabitant who left Birmingham in 1680, say, and returned forty years later would have been as astonished as his Victorian or twentieth-century counterparts.

The first Prospect of Birmingham, which was published in Dugdale's *Antiquities of Warwickshire* in 1656, depicts a little timber-framed town running up the western side of the Rea valley. Basically it is shown as a thickened and rather smudged letter 'Y'. The stem of the letter is spined by Deritend and Digbeth, the left arm by Edgbaston Street, the right by High Street and Dale End. Even the upper parts of the 'Y' are well below the tree-fringed top of the sandstone ridge. At this time the term 'High Town' still means the lower end of High Street. Only the tall spire of St. Martin's cuts the western skyline, with its weathercock able to look over the hill. Despite the fact that Birmingham's prosperity for a hundred and fifty years had depended on the 'black gold' that reached it from the west, the town itself remained entirely eastward facing.

According to Hutton, the Birmingham of Dugdale's time contained a mere fifteen streets, and many of these were not yet fully built up. By 1700 twelve new streets had been added, and by 1731 a further twenty-three, bringing the grand total up to fifty.

Prospect of Birmingham from Dugdale's Antiquities of Warwickshire, 1656.

At the Restoration, Hutton says, there had been 5,472 inhabitants and 907 houses. By 1731 there were 23,232 inhabitants and 3,719 houses. Precisely how reliable these estimates are we do not know. But clearly, in eighteenth-century terms, there had been a massive urban expansion.

Nor would anyone passing through the town in early Georgian times have had much difficulty in picking out the new from the old. For the period of accelerated growth happened to coincide with the widespread adoption of an until then little used building material, brick. So the new erections would stand out in garish red. Moreover, whereas the old sombre timber-framed houses were mainly two-storied, the recently built brick ones went up three or more floors. The visual contrast must have been every bit as stark as today's contrast between nineteenth-century brick and twentieth-century ferro-concrete. But the inhabitants — or those who mattered — apparently welcomed the change. As early as 1690 'the grey crumbling walls' of St. Martin's were 'entombed' in a brick casing; and at the same time transformed from the Gothic architectural idiom, to the Classical style that went with it. Similarly, red brick was publicly favoured in 1707 when the Grammar School in New Street was rebuilt.

The main area of development down to 1700 was between Edgbaston Street and New Street, where Birmingham's first generation of modern builders erected plain terraces of three-storied houses, using bricks made from the local Keuper Marl. It is not necessarily a judgement on the original standard of this property that a century and a half later, when the area was cleared for the building of New Street station, it was numbered among the town's grimmest slums.

Meanwhile, so urgent was the demand for workshop and domestic accommodation during the last decades of the seventeenth century, that in the old 'borough' area many of the gardens behind the long burgage plots were being filled up with densely packed buildings. As a result, by 1700, there were a hundred courts and alleys in the town, and by 1731 fifty more.

But some of the early eighteenth-century development was of a very different character. In 1697 a Mr. Pemberton, one of the town's principal merchants, purchased a piece of old priory land to the north of Bull Street and laid it out for building. The centre-piece of the resulting Priory Estate was the celebrated Old Square, designed by William Westley and built in 1713. On the other side of Bull Street, from 1711, the new church of St. Philip was arising to the Baroque design of Thomas Archer. 'The Town of Birmingham,' declared the Act of Parliament which authorized it, 'being a Market Town of great trade and commerce, was become so very populous, that, having but one

Above:
The Georgianized St. Martin's a shown on Westley's Plan, 1731.
Below:
The Old Square, from a Westley prin of 1732.

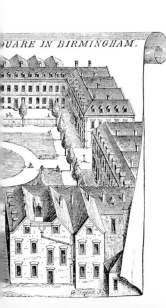

St. Philip's and its environs, from Westley's East Prospect, 1732.

Church in it, it could not contain the great part of the inhabitants . . .whereupon there should be a new Church erected and a new Churchyard set forth, and a new Parish made.' Before St. Philip's was completed, a second fashionable square was growing up around its tree-lined 4 acre churchyard. In 1726 the buildings of Temple Row were admiringly characterized as being 'as lofty and elegant and uniform as those of Bedford Row, and inhabited by People of Fortune, who were great wholesale Dealers in the Manufactures of this Town'.

Apart from St. Philips, nothing of this development survives. Fortunately, however, William Westley, who was one of the architects involved, bequeathed to posterity a full record of it – as well as of the rest of the early eighteenth-century town – in his famous Plan and East Prospect of Birmingham, published in 1731 and 1732 respectively. On the prospect the new church is drawn in exaggerated proportions, at 'the summit of the highest eminence in Birmingham'. And disposed sedately around it, we see what was in effect eighteenth-century Birmingham's own 'West End' – a top place for the top people.

Rather touchingly perhaps, Westley seems to have wanted the rest of Birmingham to be equally well-ordered and visually impressive. For he depicts the whole town as if it had just sprung up from his own drawing board – without a whisp of smoke or any hint of a blemish to be seem. But of course most of Birmingham was not like that. A traveller wrote in 1755, 'the lower part is filled with the Workshops and Warehouses of the Manufacturers, and consists chiefly of old Buildings'.

Toyshop of Europe

The topographical changes which took place in Birmingham during the late seventeenth and early eighteenth century were accompanied and paralleled by an equally remarkable transfomation of its industrial structure. 'The ancient and modern state of Birmingham', declared Hutton, 'must divide at the restoration of Charles the Second'. Down to this time, smiths were Birmingham's 'chief inhabitants', and 'the chief if not the only manufactory...was in iron'; after it 'many of the curious manufactures began to blossom'.

The making of flint-lock guns and pistols was firmly established by the early 1690s, when Birmingham gunsmiths contracted to supply 200 muskets a month to the government, and maintained this level of output throughout a seventeen-year period of war. Thereafter, the growing home demand for fowling pieces, the colonial trade — particularly with the west coast of Africa — and of course subsequent wars, all helped to consolidate small arms as a staple manufacture. During the struggle against Napoleon two-thirds of the fire-arms supplied to the army and navy were made in Birmingham. Originally Birmingham guns had to be proved in London, but in 1813 the principal gunmakers obtained Parliamentary sanction to erect the Proof House which still stands in Banbury Street.

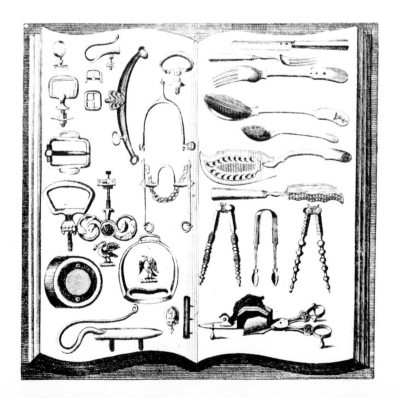

Above:
The Proof House, erected 1813.
Left:
Typical Birmingham 'toys' — from an advertisement in Wrightson's New Triennial Directory of Birmingham, 1818.

Most of Birmingham's other 'curious manufactures' were small metal articles, or 'toys' in the sense meant by Edmund Burke when he spoke of the town in 1777 as 'the great toyshop of Europe'. They ranged from metal tools and utensils, through many different kinds of household fitting, to the knick-knacks, trinkets and ornaments of what was in effect a nascent jewellery industry.

Foremost among the eighteenth-century toy trades was the making of buckles 'for hats, breeches, or shoe', until Birmingham became one of the largest suppliers in the country, with an export trade to match. 'This offspring of fancy', wrote Hutton, 'like the clouds, is ever changing . The fashion of to-day is thrown into the casting pot to-morrow'. By 1812, apparently, 'the whole generation of fashions, in the buckle line, was extinct'. But another, more durable trade, button-making, had long been growing in the town, and was ready to supersede it.

One characteristic of these new 'toy' industries was that they employed other metals than iron. Copper and brass (copper mixed with calamine) were in demand, not only for decorative work, but for the manufacture of domestic utensils. The first brass foundry was in operation by 1715, but this is assumed to have been a casting foundry, using imported metal. From about 1740, though, Turner's Brasshouse was providing local brass on a fairly large scale. Steel was a much harder metal than brass, and therefore less easy to work. Nevertheless, the fact that it did not rust and could be polished to a sparkle made it popular for ornamental objects. Small quantities of this metal were emanating from South Staffordshire in the late seventeenth century. Early in the next century at least two furnaces for converting iron into steel were established in Birmingham itself. Westley's Plan shows Carelesse's Steel House in Coleshill Street and Kettle's Steel Houses in 'White Hall or Steel-house Lane'. Meanwhile, as the eighteenth century progressed, local craftsmen made increasing use of gold, silver, tin, and various new metallic alloys: until by its end, Hutton could claim that Birmingham had added 'to her iron ornaments, the lustre of every metal . . .with all her illustrious race of compounds, heightened by fancy, and garnished with jewels'.

W. H. B. Court complained in 1938 that 'the full technical history of the Midland hardware trades . . . remains to be written'. Four decades later we still lack a detailed understanding of how Birmingham's toy industries emerged from her old-style smithery. The main tools of the traditional smith were hammer and anvil, file and grindstone. In addition to shaping, tempering, welding and sharpening, however, the new industries involved the casting, turning and later plating of metals. Even more

Kettle's Steel Houses (from Westley's Plan) and the road name that derives from them.

important was the use of dies to stamp out so-called 'battery' wares from metal sheet.

Such processes were mainly done by hand at first, but there was an increasing tendency towards mechanization. The stamping machine was replacing the die and hammer by the mid eighteenth century. Together with the press, used for cutting out blanks, this greatly speeded up the production of a wide range of articles. Similarly, although to begin with brass and other sheet was laboriously beaten out by hand, before 1750 the process had been almost entirely taken over by local rolling mills.

This was the great age of metallurgical milling in the Greater Birmingham area. Everywhere watermills were converted for industrial purposes – with windmills often being erected in their stead to grind the corn. Between twenty and thirty blade, boring, rolling and slitting mills were working along the Tame, the Rea, the Cole, and their tributaries. Part of the importance of Sarehole Mill at Hall Green lies in the fact that it is the last surviving reminder of this 'vital phase in Birmingham's industrial history'. For some years during the mid eighteenth century Sarehole served as a rolling mill, but between 1764 and 1768 it was rebuilt by Richard Eves and converted to the dual purpose of corn milling and the grinding of edge tools. It is basically this Eves mill that has been restored and opened to the public as a branch of the City Museum and Art Gallery.

But technological advances and increasingly efficient production methods are not enough by themselves to account for Birmingham's industrial growth. The early eighteenth-century merchant, Walter Tipping, was reputed 'to send away a Waggon-Load of what are called Jew's Harps at a Time'. Decisions about what sort of 'curiosities' should be made, to what designs and specifications, must have been taken by the Walter Tippings, who eventually had to sell them. Nationally, this was a period of

Left:
Sarehole Mill, looking across the mill pool. The chimney dates from the 1850s when a steam engine was installed to supplement the water power.

gradually rising living standards. The many fine country houses that were being built required furnishing with door fittings, candelabras, mirrors, silver and plated tableware; and there was a growing demand for similar, though cheaper, products on the part of farmers and the more affluent tradesmen and craftsmen of the steadily expanding towns. Not only did Birmingham merchants and factors (commission agents) corner a lion's share of this home market, they seem to have been equally successful in the ever widening fields of European and colonial trade. By the mid eighteenth century, Birmingham men were travelling regularly on the continent, even crossing the Atlantic to the West Indies and the American colonies in search of buyers.

With the steady advance of new manufactures, the older Birmingham industries declined in importance. Hutton tells us that in his time there was but 'one solitary tanner' in the town, while the leather sealers had 'no other duty but that of taking an elegant dinner'. Textile manufacture retained its importance long enough for two Birmingham immigrants, Lewis Paul and John Wyatt, to develop their ingenious spinning machine. Patented in 1738, this was put to the test at a spinning mill in the Upper Priory, using donkeys to provide the motor power. But the time and place were inappropriate, and the undertaking failed.

Meanwhile, Birmingham's original smithery crafts were not so much failing as moving out of the town itself into the domestic workshops of the surrounding villages. Above all, in the Black Country the making of nails, bits, locks, and other staple ironwares was becoming more widespread than ever. Nor did Birmingham ironmongers abandon interest in this trade. On the contrary, they intensified their efforts to control it, thereby extending Birmingham's commercial hegemony over much of South Staffordshire, and gradually establishing it as the undisputed capital of the whole 'Midland Hardware District'.

It was during the eighteenth century, too, that Birmingham's own industry began to develop the flexibility for which it has been famous ever since. The fact that its craftsmen possessed mastery over such a wide range of materials and basic techniques meant that when one line of business showed signs of failing, it was comparatively easy to switch to another.

The same technical virtuosity also encouraged experiment and innovation. Birmingham's inventors were granted ninety patents down to 1800 − over three times the number associated with its closest rival from this point of view, Manchester. Many of the originators were natives. But as the fame of Birmingham spread, it naturally began to attract inventive talent − as well as highly skilled craftsmen − from other parts. An idea might be dreamed up in Glasgow or Ayrshire, but if it involved metals,

Above:
*   workshop of Nicklin & Son, wire*
rawers and weavers, from an advert-
ement in Wrightson's Directory,
818.

Birmingham was the place to turn the dream into reality.

For the most part, the new industries were carried on, as many of their successors still are, in small workshops built at the back of dwelling houses or in converted living accommodation. But the eighteenth century, which staked out Birmingham's industrial and commercial future in so many other respects, also saw the beginning of factory production.

John Taylor — Industrial Tycoon

Birmingham's first big factory owner was John Taylor, merchant, snuff-box and button maker. As with several other key figures of the Industrial Revolution, not enough information has survived for us to fully understand and appraise the man; more than enough to have engendered a legend. Hutton, although a contemporary, speaks of Taylor in almost mythical terms:

> Him we may justly deem the Shakespeare or Newton of his day. He rose from minute beginnings, to shine in the commercial hemisphere, as they in the poetical and philosphical...To this uncommon genius we owe the gilt button, the japanned and gilt snuff-boxes, with the numerous race of enamels. From the same fountain issued the painted snuff-box...

John Taylor, 1711-75 — from miniature by W. Hedge, 1750 (b kind permission of Mr. Jonathan A Taylor).

Taylor was born about 1711, and, starting his industrial career as an ordinary artisan, he built up an extraordinary business which employed over 500 workers. Some of these may have been engaged on a domestic basis, but many undoubtedly worked in his factory, which was possibly situated in Crooked Lane, off Dale End. Suitable labour does not always seem to have been easy to find. On one occasion he is said to have sent a bell-man out into the streets of Birmingham in order to advertise job vacancies.

Lord Shelburne, a famous eighteenth-century politician who visited Taylor's works in 1766, was impressed by three things: the employment of an alloy, or 'mixed metal so mollient or ductile as easily to suffer stamping', the heavy reliance on machinery, and the way the division of labour was used to speed up production:

> Thus a button passes through fifty hands, and each hand perhaps passes a thousand a day; likewise, by this means, the work becomes so simple that, five times in six, children of six to eight years old do it as well as men, and earn from ten pence (4p.) to eight shillings (40p.) a week.

Taylor used three distinct processes in the finishing and decorating of his wares: gilt plating, which he is himself thought to have introduced into Birmingham, japanning or enamelling, and painting. One employee regularly earned £3.10s.(£3.50) per week by painting 3,360 snuff boxes at the rate of a farthing each (10 for 1p.).

As a businessman Taylor's gifts included 'ingenuity in mechanical inventions', a flair for organization and management, shrewd commercial insight, and above all, the knack of finding markets for enormous quantities of mass produced goods. In a town that had known nothing but small craftsmen and small workshops before, it was no doubt the sheer scale of his operations that staggered contemporaries. The value of the buttons alone which came from his shop could amount to £800 per week, while one aristocrat paid 80 guineas (£84) for a single 'toy'.

Another Taylor venture was the founding, with Sampson Lloyd II, of Birmingham's first bank. The town had long been a centre of capital, providing money not only for local enterprises, but for neighbouring districts, including the coal mines and iron works of the Black Country. Indeed, Hutton tells us that before 1765 'about every tenth trader was a banker, or retailer of cash'.

Sampson Lloyd I had come to Birmingham from Wales in 1698 and quickly built up a flourishing business in the iron trade, which included what was probably the town's first slitting mill. It was this man's son and namesake who was John Taylor's principal partner in the setting up of Taylors & Lloyds Bank. This opened its doors at Dale End in 1765 and was to outlast Taylor's manufacturing business by many a long day. For it was the predecessor of what, since 1865 — after the withdrawal of the Taylor family — has been known as Lloyds Bank.

At his death in 1775, John Taylor left a private residence at Bordesley on which he had spent £10,000, extensive landed estates in Yardley, Sheldon, Coleshill and several other rural parishes, and a total fortune of £200,000.

Among the few personal memorials of this first Birmingham tycoon are three account books in the Birmingham Reference Library. On one page we find him paying £8.8s.(£8.40) to 'Polly Dalton for Lond(on) Journey'; on another investing £60 in 'the Elmdom Turnpike'. But more evocatively, on page 37 of the first volume there is a mysterious jotting concerning 'aq fortis, oyl vitrol, Glober Salts, Gilt mettle', etc.

Left, above:
Wall plaque in Dale End.
Left: Sampson Lloyd II (by kind permission of Lloyds Bank).

The Soho Works

Although Lord Shelburne described Mr. Taylor in 1766 as Birmingham's 'most established manufacturer and trader', he also noted that others 'were beginning to rival him in the extent of his trade'. Among these was John Baskerville (1706-75), who established a lucrative japanning business at Easy Hill, before turning his creative energies to the printing press for which he became so renowned. Hutton tells us that he was 'fond of show', adorned his figure with gold lace, and rode about the town in a japanned carriage 'each panel of which was a distinct picture', so that it 'might be considered the *pattern card of his trade*'. Having worked for many years in perfecting paper and ink, as well as designing, cutting and casting nine founts of type, Baskerville published his first book, *The Poems of Vergil*, in 1757. The following year he was appointed Printer to the Cambridge University Press: which enabled him to bring out editions of 'Paradise Lost, the Bible, Common Prayer, Roman and English Classics, etc. . . . with more satisfaction to the literary world than emolument to himself'. Within twenty years of Baskerville's interment in the mausoleum he had erected at Easy Hill, his elegant type face had been largely forgotten. But since its reintroduction by Stanley Morison in 1926, 'Baskerville type' has been extensively used throughout the English speaking world.

John Baskerville.

Baskerville's 'invention', says Hutton, 'was of the true Birmingham model, active'. And so was that of his gifted apprentice, Henry Clay. He patented what became known as 'papier mâché' in 1772, and eventually had a factory of 300 people turning out 'tables, cabinets, teatrays, caddies, panels for doors' from that unlikely material. But foremost among John Taylor's trading rivals was Matthew Boulton, who had founded the Soho Works just two years prior to Lord Shelburne's visit.

Plaque in Steelhouse Lane, over looking Snow Hill.

Boulton was born in 1728 into the family of a small Birmingham buckle and button maker. The business was already flourishing when the father (also called Matthew) took his son into partnership in 1749, and charged him with its management. But it must have seemed a puny affair compared with John Taylor's splendid undertaking; and consciously or unconsciously, Boulton appears to have set his heart upon emulating or even surpassing 'the Esquire', as he always respectfully called Taylor. What was required, he decided, was a business in which control could be exercised over the entire industrial process, from the preparation of raw materials

Matthew Boulton.

to the manufacture and marketing of the widest possible variety of finished articles.

The original premises, near Snow Hill, was inadequate for this purpose, so one of the first problems was to find an alternative site. In 1755 and 1756 the Boultons, father and son, acquired Sarehole Mill (see page 52) and the adjacent Sarehole Farm in the manor of Yardley. But although Boulton probably rolled his own sheet metal here for six years, and although the two holdings together would seem to have offered ample space for additional workshops, for some reason, this first choice proved unsuitable. The water supply may have been disappointing; or perhaps Sarehole was just too far away from the South Staffordshire coal field.

Whatever the causes, in 1761-2 Boulton made a second move, this time to Handsworth Heath, where at a place already called Soho, on the Hockley Brook, he was able to acquire another small mill, similar to Sarehole, with a substantial piece of recently enclosed heathland attached. An additional advantage of this site was that it was served by the turnpike road from Wednesbury, along which coal and other supplies could be brought quickly and cheaply.

At Soho Boulton seems to have had yet another false start. For originally all he did was demolish and replace the small mill. It was not until 1764, after the death of his first wife who had brought him a substantial fortune, and after he had taken a Birmingham merchant, John Fothergill, into partnership, that he eventually mustered the capital to build the infinitely more ambitious Soho Works. This stood on the Hockley Brook at Handsworth, near the point where it is crossed by Factory Road. Swinney's Birmingham Directory for 1774 contains a good description of the manufactory itself, and how Boulton was using it ten years after its opening:

The Soho Works, as represented in Wrightson's Directory of Birmingham, 1839.

ESTABLISHED. 1764.

The building consists of four squares, with shops, warehouses, etc., for a Thousand Workmen, who, in a great variety of Branches, excel in their several Departments; not only in the fabrication of Buttons, Buckles, Boxes, Trinkets, etc. . . . but in many other Arts . . . The number of ingenious mechanical Contrivances they avail themselves of, by the means of Water Mills, much facilitates their Work, and saves a great portion of Time and Labour . . . Their excellent ornamental pieces have been admired by the Nobility and Gentry, not only of this Kingdom but all Europe: and are allowed to surpass anything of the kind made abroad.

Clearly, Soho was very different from the 'dark Satanic mills' of the North. Unlike textile manufacture, Birmingham industry was to remain predominantly workshop based for a century and more to come. Instead of being a 'mill' in the northern sense, or a 'factory' in the modern sense, Soho was a collection of workshops, where teams of highly skilled craftsmen pursued separate specialisms; but where a whole range of basic facilities were rationalized and made available to all sections. Thus there were stores from which the necessary raw materials could be drawn, design rooms where new projects could be planned, common warehousing facilities for the full range of finished products, a common advertising and marketing department, and − in the side-wings of the factory − even workmen's dwellings. Above all, there was a common Master, who had sufficient character, imagination and integrity to be able to imbue the whole enterprise with a common philosophy.

From the start, Boulton resolved to found the reputation of Soho on jewellery, silver and plated goods of the highest quality. 'I am very desirous of becoming a *great silversmith*', he once wrote. The many fine examples of his work in the Birmingham Museum and elsewhere leave no doubt that he, and the designers he attracted to Soho, possessed that supreme eighteenth-century virtue, 'taste'. Indeed, Boulton was as much an exponent and patron of the arts, as he was an engineer and

Birmingham has over a dozen 'Mill *street names, but only one Factory* *Road. This once led to its most* *renowned factory, the Soho Manufac**tory.*

Below/Left:
Silver sauce tureen, made by Boulton *and Fothergill in 1776. (The Birming**ham Assay Office).*
Right:
The present-day Assay Office in *Newhall Street. The original office* *was in Little Cannon Street.*

businessman. In this sense, Soho became the Etruria of Birmingham, and Boulton its Wedgwood. So it was appropriate that he should have led the other silversmiths of the town in the agitation which in 1773 obtained for Birmingham its own Assay Office.

But Boulton also set himself the task of capturing mass markets, and for this he had to produce goods as cheaply as possible and in quantity. Down to his time the Birmingham toy trade had tended to operate in such a way that 'cheap' often meant 'gaudy', 'throw-away', 'shoddy'. The Soho philosophy simply refused to accept this equation. Boulton insisted that every one of his products, however inexpensive, should be of the best design, material and workmanship that could possibly be achieved at the price.

The same integrity was apparent in Boulton's relationship with his workers. 'As the Smith cannot do without his Striker', he told them as an old man, 'so neither can the Master do without his Workmen'. And again, 'good, honest, and faithful workmen . . . I have always considered as classed with my best friends'. However patronizing this may sound to twentieth-century ears, it was at least preferable to the gruffer noises being made by many of his contemporaries. Moreover, to some extent at least, the words were backed by action. At a time when pauper children were regularly apprenticed at seven, Boulton refused to employ any child under twelve. He had the inside of workshops whitewashed regularly to ensure light and cleanliness, and took particular care over ventilation. Even more unusual was his introduction in 1792 of a social insurance scheme, with wage-related payments and benefits.

As a businessman, Boulton's greatest strength, perhaps, was his intense awareness of the world around him. He took tremendous pains to keep himself informed as to markets. To a business agent he wrote of his 'wish to know the taste, ye fashions, ye toys, both usefull & ornamental, the impliments, vessells, &c &c &c that prevail in all ye different parts of Europe, as I should be glad to work for all Europe'. He was no less eager to keep abreast of scientific and technological possibilities:

> If in ye Course of your future travelling you can pick up for me any Metallick oars or fossell Substances or any other curious Natural productions I should be much Obliged to you as I am fond of all those things that have a tendency to improve my knowledge in Mechanick Arts in which my Manufactory will every Year become more & more general . . .

There was more than a mind-narrowing quest for mere profit here. And it was this openness to new ideas that was soon to make Soho, not only a manufactory, but a seat of invention.

Boulton, Watt and Murdock

'I shall never forget Mr. Boulton's expression to me', wrote Boswell after a visit to Soho, ' "I sell here, Sir, what all the world desires to have – POWER" '. Although James Watt invented the steam engine, it was Boulton who best appreciated its revolutionary significance, had the 'Brummy' nerve to back his judgement, and the intensity of commitment needed to convert others to the same point of view. In a sense, the Soho man's missionary zeal was a product and generalization of his own experience. Within a year or two of establishing the manufactory, he had found it necessary to install a second water wheel, and then a horse mill, in an effort to keep his own machinery turning. His initial interest in Watt's steam pump, when the two first met in 1768, was simply that such an engine at Soho would enable him to pump back water from his tail race to the mill pool, and so re-use the precious, power-giving liquid again and again. However, when a little later, Watt's first partner, John Roebuck, found himself running into financial difficulties, Boulton at once offered to switch all available resources to the development of the new invention. He wrote to Watt in 1769 proposing the establishment of a special factory for that purpose:

> . . . my idea was to settle a manufactory near to my own by the side of our canal where I would erect all the conveniences necessary for the completion of the engines and from which manufactory we would serve all the world with engines of all sizes.

In the event, the trade depression of the early 1770s found Boulton himself in serious financial difficulties, and it was to be another twenty-four years before the special manufactory was built. Nevertheless, the Boulton and Watt partnership was sealed in 1774 and the great engineer moved to Birmingham where he was to stay for the rest of his life.

Watt's first separate condenser pumping engine had been erected at Kinneal, Scotland in 1769, the year in which he also took out the patent. Boulton's opening sales drive was on the South Staffordshire and East Shropshire coalfields, where a number of Watt's steam pumps were installed in the late 1770s. Among the first half-dozen, too, was that built in 1777 for the Birmingham Canal Navigation at Smethwick. Moved to Ocker Hill in 1895, this, the oldest extant Watt engine, is now preserved in the Birmingham Museum of Science and Industry. But the main market for steam pumps soon became the copper and tin mines of Cornwall, where William Murdock, another Scottish recruit to the firm, spent nineteen years supervising their installation.

The Boulton, Watt and Murdock memorial, Broad Street, erected in 1956.

100 h.p. Boulton and Watt double acting rotary engine, said to have been installed at the Fazeley Street brass rolling mills, Birmingham in the 1780s

Watt's first engine was ideal for draining mines. But Boulton was a factory, not a colliery owner; so from his point of view it was only a half-way house. What is more, he was convinced that the industrial world at large was eagerly awaiting a steam engine that would turn machinery. Ironically, Watt himself was much less optimistic. When Boulton wrote to him suggesting that the cotton mills would provide a ready market, he replied damply that Lancashire had so much water power that the use of steam would be uneconomic. However, in 1782 Watt's epoch-making Rotary Steam Engine was patented, and its reception was every bit as enthusiastic as Boulton had foretold.

Only a year later, we find Charles Twigg's steam mill at Snow Hill advertising the supply of power for the rolling of metals, the grinding and boring of gun barrels, 'the polishing of steel goods, finishing of Buckles, Buckle Chapes and a variety of other articles usually done by foot lathes'. 'The whole is worked by Steam Engine', the advertisement proudly continued, 'and saves Manufacturers the trouble of sending several miles into the country to water mills'. Before the eighteenth century was out at least six other 'Fire Engines' were at work in Birmingham; and orders were reaching Soho in steadily mounting numbers from industrial enterprises throughout the country.

1797 'cartwheel' penny, minted at Soho.

Having successfully midwifed the rotary engine, Boulton's overriding passion during the mid-eighties was to apply it to the manufacture of coinage. The quantity of British coins at this time was so inadequate and the quality so inferior that counterfeiting − much of it done in Birmingham − was a profitable occupation. Boulton realized that this evil could only be eliminated by producing official coins in such numbers and of such perfection that the making of fakes would cease to be worthwhile. Designing the necessary machinery himself, by 1788 he had six steam-driven coining presses at work in a new purpose-built section of the manufactory known as the Soho Mint. The government was indifferent at first. But after several years of minting overseas currencies and trade tokens − themselves a product of the coin shortage − Boulton was at last awarded a Crown contract. The result was the superb 1797-99 George III issue of 'cartwheel' pennies and two-penny pieces, over 45 million of which were minted at Soho in two years.

Originally, components for both Watt's steam engines had been manufactured elsewhere, the engines then being assembled *in situ* by Soho engineers. By the 1790s, however, the engine business had become so booming that the special engine factory,

which Boulton had always had in mind, could at last be built. This was sited on the Birmingham-Wolverhampton canal, about a mile from the Soho Works. According to *Aris's Gazette*, the opening ceremonies, which were held on 30th January 1796, included a 'Rearing Feast' given to the engine smiths, and all the other workmen employed in the erection:

> When dinner was over, the Founder of Soho entered, and consecrated this new branch of it, by sprinkling the walls with wine, and then, in the name of Vulcan, and all the Gods and Goddesses of *Fire* and *Water*, pronounced the name of it SOHO FOUNDRY, and all the people cried *Amen*. . . . A Ball, with tea, was given in the evening to Venus and the Graces . . .

Six years later there was another bout of junketing at Soho, when the Manufactory was illuminated in celebration of the short-lived Peace of Amiens. Amidst the many oil lamps which decorated the front of the building were the first two gas lights ever to appear in public. The development of gas lighting was one of the pioneer ventures of the third member of the great Soho triumvirate, William Murdock. During his early years in Cornwall, Murdock had concentrated on the design and making of the model locomotive which demonstrated for the first time in this country that steam could be used to propel a vehicle. Unfortunately, this invention came at a time when the development of Watt's rotary engine was already stretching the resources of Soho to the limit. Murdock was a deferential employee and the two partners had little difficulty in persuading him to drop the project, thereby missing for Soho the 'hat-trick' of pioneering all three basic types of steam engine. However, Murdock's experiments with gas were better received, and by 1805 gas lighting plant was becoming one of the major products of the foundry.

From 1765, or a little before, the myriad-sided Matthew Boulton had been the chief mentor of an informal group of outstanding businessmen, scientists and intellectuals, which, largely through his inspiration, became a kind of hot-house of new and stimulating ideas; or 'a pilot project for the Industrial Revolution'. By 1776 this group was known as the Lunar Society, a name which derived from the fact that meetings — at the homes of different members in turn — were usually held on or near the day of a full moon, so making it relatively easy for those attending to find their way home afterwards. Apart from Boulton and Watt, industrialists belonging to the Lunar Society included John Baskerville, Samuel Galton, the Quaker gunmaker, James Keir, the glass and chemical manufacturer, and Josiah Wedgwood, the master potter. Then there were several physicians, like Dr. William Withering, of Edgbaston Hall, the man who first established the possibilities of digitalis

as a heart stimulant; and Dr. Erasmus Darwin, botanist, philosopher and poet, whose obsession with 'the struggle for existence' made him a progenitor, not only of Charles Darwin — his grandson — but of the Theory of Evolution. But perhaps the intellectually most distinguished member was Joseph Priestley, minister of the Unitarian New Meeting House in Birmingham from 1780-91, who, as the discoverer of oxygen, nitrogen, ammonia and sulphuric acid, is generally regarded as 'the father of modern chemistry'. 'Dear Boulton,' wrote Erasmus Darwin in April 1778, 'I am sorry the infernal divinities who visit mankind with diseases and are therefore at perpetual war with doctors, should have prevented my seeing all your great men at Soho today. Lord! what inventions, what wit, what rhetoric, metaphysical, mechanical and pyrotechnical, will be on the wing, bandied like a shuttlecock from one to another of your troop of philosophers! while poor I, I by myself, I, imprisoned in a post-chaise, am jogged and jostled, and bumped and bruised along the King's high-road, to make war upon a stomach-ache or a fever!'

The Soho Works was demolished in 1862-3. But the Soho Foundry, although much altered by W & T Avery Ltd. who took it over in 1895, still has remnants of the original premises, including some workmen's cottages, traces of the canal wharves, and of an early gasometer. On Soho Hill, hidden away behind late-Victorian housing, Soho House, where the Lunar Society so often met, is now used as residential quarters by the Police. St. Mary's Handsworth contains a wonderful group of memorials to the three great men. Finally, the twentieth century has paid its tribute with an over life-size conversation piece of the Soho triumvirate in Broad Street, beside which Registry Office newly-weds often have their photographs taken. But for Soho they might not be flocking there in such numbers.

Memorials in St. Mary's Church, Handsworth: James Watt (left), William Murdock (below), Matthew Boulton (right).
Far right:
Soho House.

The 'Silver Cross'

Down to the eighteenth century it was arguably to Birmingham's long-term advantage that, lacking a navigable river, it suffered from poor communications. The rise to pre-eminence of its metal industries could well have owed something to this deficiency. For the costliness of road carriage must have been one of the factors which encouraged Birmingham craftsmen to make as much as possible out of as little as possible: or in other words, to minimize their use of raw materials but maximize their skill.

However, despite this frugality, as the town grew and its industrial activity intensified, the traffic in raw materials and finished products assumed ever greater proportions. The roads leading from the Black Country 'daily presented the curious feature of an almost unending procession of carts and waggons bringing the supplies needed by our manufacturers'. Road improvement helped. The roads to Stratford (and London), Warwick, Bromsgrove, Wednesbury and Walsall had all been turnpiked by 1730; those to Coventry (and London), Stourbridge, Dudley and Alcester by 1770. Yet turnpiking, while improving the speed and increasing the reliability of road transport, did little to reduce its cost. Goods sent by packhorse to London were charged at a rate of £7-9 per ton, to Liverpool and Bristol at £5.

It is hardly surprising that when 'a meeting of Inhabitants' was called in January 1767 'to consult about making a Navigable Cut . . . to run as near as possible thro' the Center of the Colleries', that 'it was unanimously agreed to have it Survey'd'.

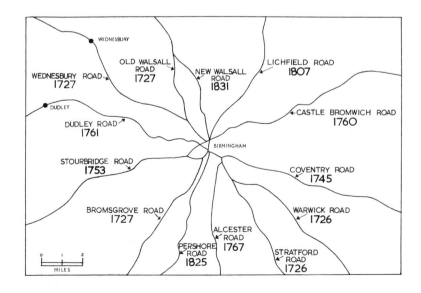

Turnpike roads from Birmingham with dates of turnpiking.

Top:
The Birmingham Canal Office,
Paradise Street in 1830.
Above:
Warehousing on the Birmingham
Canal, photographed from Brasshouse
Passage.

By August of the same year £50,000 had been raised in shares, and James Brindley's plan for a canal from Birmingham to Wolverhampton had been approved. By February 1768 the necessary Act of Parliament had been passed. And a mere twenty-one months after that, on 6th November 1769, the canal's first ten miles, running from the Wednesbury colleries to the wharf off Paradise Street, was opened. There was much public rejoicing:

> What mortals so happy as *Birmingham* Boys?
> What people so flush'd with the sweetest of joys?
> All hearts fraught with mirth at the Wharf shall appear,
> Their aspects proclaim it the Jubilee year.

> Then revel in gladness, let harmony flow,
> From the district of *Bordesley* to *Paradise Row*.
> For true feeling joy in each breast must be wrought,
> *When Coals under Five-pence per hundred are bought.*

This was the retail price. Coal had before been selling from 15s. (75p.) to 18s. (90p.) per ton wholesale; by May 1770 it had fallen to 4s. (20p.) per ton. During the 'canal mania' of the next fifty years an intricate network of waterways was constructed through and about Birmingham, and into every corner of the Black Country. Matthew Boulton, 'one of the most active promoters of the original scheme' – prior to siting the Soho Foundry on the Birmingham Canal – had had a branch canal and wharf constructed to serve the Soho Works. Other industrialists followed suit, until long stretches of canal bank were lined with warehouses, workshops and factories. 'This watery passage,' wrote Hutton, 'exclusive of loading the proprietors with wealth, tends greatly to the improvement of some branches of trade, by introducing heavy materials at a small expence, such as pig iron for the foundries, lime-stone, articles for the manufacture of brass and steel, stone, brick, slate, timber, &c.' The brass industry was a particular beneficiary. Ensured of cheap raw materials, brass foundries were built on the banks of the canal north of Broad Street (where Brasshouse Passage is still to be found); and by the end of the century brass had become one of the leading manufactures of the town.

From the beginning Birmingham businessmen looked for a two-fold benefit from canals. Not only would they facilitate the cheap and convenient movement of basic supplies within the manufacturing district itself; just as importantly, they could be used to connect Birmingham to the chief national waterways. The extension of the Birmingham Canal to Autherley in 1772 gave access to the Staffordshire & Worcestershire Canal, completed in the same year, and thence to Bristol

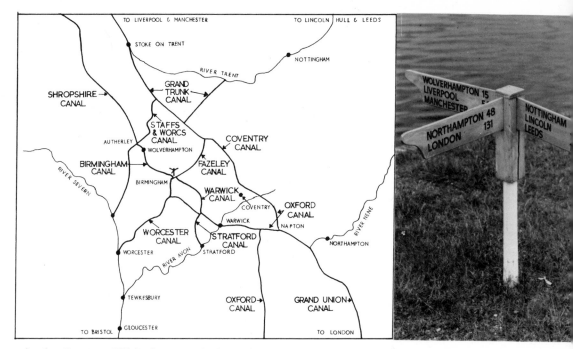

The map contains the following labels:

TO LIVERPOOL & MANCHESTER · TO LINCOLN HULL & LEEDS · STOKE ON TRENT · NOTTINGHAM · RIVER TRENT · GRAND TRUNK CANAL · SHROPSHIRE CANAL → · STAFFS & WORCS CANAL · AUTHERLEY · WOLVERHAMPTON · COVENTRY CANAL · BIRMINGHAM CANAL → · FAZELEY CANAL · BIRMINGHAM · RIVER SEVERN · WARWICK CANAL · COVENTRY · OXFORD CANAL · NAPTON · RIVER NENE · WORCESTER CANAL · WARWICK · STRATFORD CANAL · STRATFORD · NORTHAMPTON · WORCESTER · RIVER AVON · TEWKESBURY · OXFORD CANAL → · GRAND UNION CANAL → · TO BRISTOL · GLOUCESTER · TO LONDON

via the Severn. With the completion of the Grand Trunk Canal in 1777, access was gained to Liverpool via the Mersey, and Hull via the Trent and Humber. The Birmingham & Fazeley Canal (opened 1789) considerably shortened routes to the northern ports; the Worcester & Birmingham Canal (opened 1815) cut down the travelling time to Bristol. Meanwhile, with the opening of the Warwick & Birmingham Canal in 1799, and its extension to Napton on the Oxford Canal, Birmingham obtained a direct canal link with London.

By the mid nineteenth century the Birmingham Canal Navigations, which from 1848 incorporated all the Black Country canals, had become the hub of the national canal system. Once again, Birmingham had secured, not merely a fair reward for its enterprise and initiative, but a generous bonus of 'Brummy luck'. Having started off with no other waterway than the spindly Rea, it now found itself at the centre of Brindley's 'Silver Cross'. The original shares in the B.C.N. are reckoned to have cost £140 each; by 1792 they were worth £1,110.

During the last twenty years Birmingham has again become canal conscious: though this time with leisure and amenity in mind, rather than coal and profit. A section of the Birmingham & Fazeley Canal, known as the 'James Brindley Walk', has been cleared and renovated; and the Gas Street Basin – although its surrounding warehouses have been shamefully demolished – is also to be preserved. On Saturday 1st November 1969, a

Left:
The Midland Canal network.
Above:
Signpost at Farmer's Bridge can[al] junction (north of the Gas Str[eet] Basin).

The Gas Street Canal Basin, looking north.

66

dozen boats belonging to the B.C.N. Society chugged their ponderous way from Birmingham to Wednesbury in commemoration of one of Birmingham's most significant bi-centenaries.

Greater Birmingham in the Eighteenth Century

It cannot be emphasized too often that until industrial and technological pioneers like Boulton and Watt opened the way for a massive exploitation of coal, iron and other mineral resources, there was a strict limit to the number of people Britain, or any part of it, could possibly support. Indeed, this harsh fact was demonstrated in the Birmingham area only a generation before the Industrial Revolution began to gather momentum.

During the three years 1727-9 people were dying at a faster rate in local villages than had perhaps been the case at any time since the Black Death. At Yardley – a parish of about 1,100 people – burials, which had averaged 26 per annum over the previous decade, soared three-fold to 71 and 88 in the years 1727 and 1728 respectively. Work on the Five Parishes (see page 41) suggests that the crisis began with a severe dearth – if not famine – in the autumn of 1727. And this was followed by two further years of dear bread, accompanied by influenza and other epidemics.

The resulting suffering is plain from the Yardley poor law accounts. William Hopkins was gaoled in 1726, leaving his wife with three young children to support. From Easter 1727 to easter 1728 Susan Hopkins's weekly poor law allowances varied from 1s. 6d. to 2s. 6d. and amounted to £5. 17s. (£5.85) in all. This was at a time when the farm labourer's wage – which Susan lacked – was 7d. to 8d. per day, or about £9.50 per annum, while corn was double its normal price. In the spring of 1728 the parish increased the Hopkins's weekly pay to 3s. 0d. But this 'generosity' was either too little or too late. On 26 August 6s. 6d. was spent on the burial of Mary, one of Susan's children. On 21 April 1729 Susan herself was buried. And although the overseers found no less than £8.10s. (£8.50) to support the remaining children in that poor law year, a son died in January 1730. This left one member of the family – apart from the gaoled William – to tell the story of these catastrophic years. Nor was the situation necessarily much better for families which had their breadwinner at home. The poor relief paid to William Phillips rose to 5s. 0d. per week during 1727-8. Yet

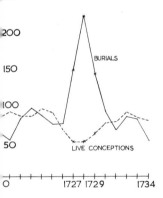

Burials and live conceptions in three Arden parishes (Yardley, Sheldon, Solihull), by harvest year (August-July), 1720-34.

67

Thomas, son of William Phillips, was buried on 7 May 1728 at the parish expense, followed by his father on 18 August of the same year. Meanwhile another son had been 'got off the books' by being 'bound apprentice'.

However, locally at least, the years 1727-9 seem to have been a watershed so far as the balance between population and resources is concerned. Not only were there no further 'crises of subsistence', but we soon find that people are managing to marry earlier and have larger families than ever before. Thus, during the period 1700-24 five-parish women had entered wedlock at an average age of 27.5 years and borne an average of 3.1 children. Their counterparts for 1775-99 married almost 3 years younger (24.6 years) and had an average of 4.3 children.

Not unnaturally, these changes in family habits led to steady population growth: until by 1801 the five parishes together had some 5,500 souls, which represented a 60% advance on the 1740 figure of about 3,400. A comparison of the five-parish population graph with that of Birmingham suggests that this growth accompanied – or rather, perhaps, followed and echoed – that of Birmingham itself. Nor is it difficult to see why. The proximity of an ever-expanding industrial town must have improved the economic circumstances of local parishes in many ways. The fact that there was a greedy market for farm produce within a few miles would have stimulated farmers, not only to cultivate every available acre, but to adopt the various agricultural improvements that were then in vogue. Just as importantly, Birmingham's appetite for 'outwork' must have encouraged industrial activity. By 1841 at least 330 households in the five parishes were exclusively dependent on manufacturing crafts. Meanwhile, those unable to find work locally could be sure of doing so a few miles away. We know that from about 1750 many pauper children were being apprenticed to Birmingham masters. And for every parish apprentice, there were doubtless another ten youngsters who moved into Birmingham of their own accord, or at the behest of their parents.

The register of immigrants kept by the Birmingham authorities from 1686 to 1726 shows that 224 out of 715 newcomers – or almost a third – came from Greater Birmingham parishes. Hutton tells us that by his time the town was attracting immigrants from 50 miles around; and some of its most illustrious sons came from even further afield. Nevertheless the inflow of local immigrants must have continued to increase – in absolute, if not in relative terms – throughout the eighteenth and early nineteenth centuries.

In fact, at this stage the rural parishes of Greater

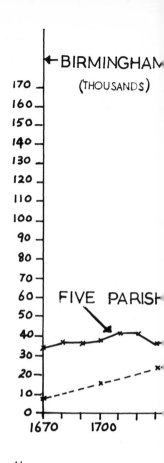

Above:
Population of Birmingham and Five Arden Parishes, 1670-1831.
Below:
All over Greater Birmingham, eighteenth-century population growth led to the erection of squatters' cottages on late-surviving wastes and commons. This one, formerly on Billesley Common, now serves the Moseley Golf Club. The back view is more revealing than the front, since it shows how the meagre accommodation was extended by the addition of a rear lean-to or 'outshut'.

68

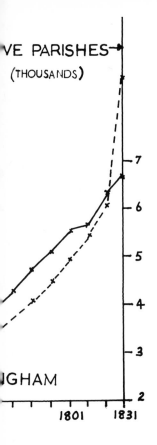

— 7

— 6

— 5

— 4

— 3

IGHAM

— 2

1801   1831

NEWHALL ST 3

New Hall, as shown on Westley's Prospect, 1732, with the street name that derives from it.

Birmingham were serving, both as a granary for the industrial town, and as a breeding ground and nursery for a considerable proportion of its industrial labour.

Georgian Estates and Suburbs

Birmingham's rapid population growth — from about 23,000 in 1731 to 170,000 in 1831 — generated an equally rapid topographical expansion; and this produced a completely different type of urban environment from that found in the older parts of the town. The new pattern was beginning to emerge by 1731, when Westley's Plan shows that to the east of their fashionable Old Square, the Pembertons had developed such streets as John Street, Newton Street and Thomas Street, with a more modest type of tenant in mind. Similarly, the presence on the same plan of Slaney Street, Wearman Street and Whithall Street, to the north of Steelhouse Lane, tells us that the Wearman estate was under development. Having provided the core of the Gun Quarter for a century or so, this last — like the Pemberton estate — has now been swept away. But much of the northern part of the adjacent Newhall estate still serves as the core of the Jewellery Quarter.

The Newhall, or Colmore, estate was a speculative venture of the ancient Colmore family, who, although no longer residing here, still owned a roughly rectangular block of about 100 acres on the north-western edge of early eighteenth-century Birmingham, together with several smaller parcels elsewhere. More or less at the centre of their main holding stood the Jacobean family mansion known as New Hall, with a long straight avenue leading up to it from Colmore Row. Today the line of this avenue is indicated by Newhall Street; and from 1746 the Colmores began laying out a regular grid pattern of streets across the park land on either side of it, at the same time dividing up the resulting rectangles of building land into leasehold plots of various sizes. The actual houses were erected by the purchasers. But some attempt was made to control building standards, since the 120 year leases generally specified, not only that buildings were to be in a straight line and of three storeys, but a minimum construction cost.

Properties had been built along Colmore Row and what is now Edmund Street by 1750, while Hanson's 1778 Plan of Birmingham shows Great Charles Street largely, and Lionel Street partially, built up; with a further as yet vacant extension of the street grid, centred on St Paul's Square, beyond. The

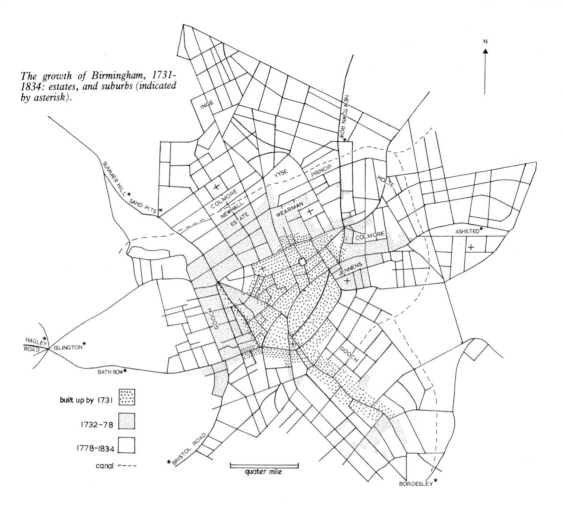

The growth of Birmingham, 1731-1834: estates, and suburbs (indicated by asterisk).

N

INGE

NEW TOWN ROW*

SUMMER HILL*

SAND PITS*

VYSE

PRINCIP

HOLTE

COLMORE

NEWHALL ESTATE

WEARMAN

COLMORE

ASHSTED*

JENNENS

GOOCH

GOOCH

HAGLEY ROAD*

ISLINGTON*

BATH ROW*

built up by 1731

1732-78

1778-1834

canal ----

BRISTOL ROAD*

quater mile

BORDESLEY*

provision of St Paul's, which was consecrated in 1779, was regarded as an essential part of the development, if only because ready access to a place of worship increased property values. Accordingly, as well as donating 3 acres for the church and cemetery, the Colmores gave £1,000 towards the building of the former. By the 1780s, too, the Fazeley Canal was being dug through the northern part of the estate, and this was welcomed as a further rent-enhancing factor.

From the start, the Newhall estate prospered. Its great size meant that the last plots were not taken up until the early nineteenth century. But small manufacturers of buckles, buttons, jewellery and steel toys were only too anxious — directly they could afford it — to abandon 'irregular foul-smelling buildings' in the old parts of the town and 'erect . . . one or more good substantial dwelling houses with the proper and necessary outbuildings' on the Newhall estate.

Meanwhile, the development of the Wearman estate was

continuing, together with other Colmore land and areas belonging to the Lench Trust, the Princip, Jennens and Holte (later Dartmouth) families to the north-east of the town, and the old manorial lands of the Gooch family to the west. As with the Colmores, new streets were laid out as far as possible in regular grid patterns, while purchasers of building plots were offered long leases of 120 or 99 years and required to erect their own properties. As with the Colmores, too, both the Jennens and Wearman families provided a new church as the focal point of their estate, the Jennens's St Bartholomew's being commenced in 1749 and the Wearman's St Mary's in 1774. 'Wherever a chapel is erected', wrote Hutton, 'the houses, as if touched by the wand of magic, spring into existence'.

Only on the south-east side of the town does development seem to have been difficult to instigate. In 1771 land here was being offered to let by Henry Bradford — after whom Bradford Street was named — at ¾d. per square yard, while sites in the north-west were fetching twice that rate. And indeed, four years previously the same landowner had promised 'a freehold to the man who should first build upon his estate'. Yet the main inhibiting factor, poor communications, was no more than temporary; and from the 1780s, with the prospect of the Warwick Canal entering the district, 'there was a massive occupation of land by builders'.

Many of the houses erected on the Newhall estate and elsewhere were solid brick and slate merchant houses, but others were of inferior quality from the beginning. 'The proprietor generally contracts for a house of certain dimensions, at a stipulated price', Hutton tells us, but 'this induces the artist to use some ingredients of the cheaper kind, and sometimes to try whether he can cement the materials with *sand*, instead of lime'. Unfortunately also, the pressure on accommodation and the financial attractions for a small businessman of sub-letting, often led to the speedy deterioration of even the better properties. Upper rooms were let off as workshops, while other 'shopping' or 'blind-back' workmen's houses were built up against what had originally been the back garden wall. 'Whithall Street, near Steelhouse Lane', reads an advertisement of 1826, 'Two houses, numbers 33 and 34, for sale. Range of shopping behind, three stories high, and a court of five dwellings with a large yard, entry, pump and brewhouse, and offices'. In fact, so widespread did this habit of court development become that before long housing standards on the eighteenth-century estates were often little better than in Deritend or Digbeth. Eight local doctors reported in 1836 that there were 2,030 courts containing 12,254 tenements in

the town and that these housed most of the working population.

It is hardly surprising that late eighteenth-century observers were already declaring that 'Birmingham is not a place gentlemen would chuse to make a residence'. Apart from its 'close population', among other disadvantages noted by contemporaries, were 'the noxious effusion of various metallic trades and above all the continual smoke arising from the immense quantity of coals consumed'. (By 1836 there were 169 steam engines at work in Birmingham.) Given this environmental deterioration, many of the merchants, manufacturers and professional men who had once been content to live in the Old Square or Temple Row inevitably began looking for alternative accommodation.

Among the first to move out of town were John Taylor, Birmingham's first big factory owner, and Sampson Lloyd II, the man with whom he founded Taylors and Lloyds Bank. Both acquired land at Bordesley in the mid eighteenth century, the former rebuilding Bordesley Hall and the latter erecting a fine Georgian mansion known as The Farm, Sparkbrook. Joseph Priestley also lived here from 1780 to 1791, while in 1781 Hutton listed Camp Hill (Bordesley) as one of the 'five clumps of houses belonging to Birmingham, which may be denoted hamlets'. There were then 31 houses; and a number of these still stand – including the architecturally and historically important Lloyd house, albeit in a sadly neglected condition.

Hutton's other hamlets 'belonging to Birmingham', or early suburbs, were 'at the Sand-pits upon the Dudley-road', with 14 houses; 'one furlong from Exeter-row' (i.e., along Bath Row), with 34; Islington (near Five Ways), with 29; and

72

Walmer Lane (or New Town Row) on the road to Aston, with 17. Thereafter, the 'Summer Hill Estate' was announced in 1790 as having been staked out 'for a range of elegant and uniform building, comprising fifteen houses, along the declivity of a beautiful hill'. And at about the same time Ashsted was being developed as a planned suburb, north of Vauxhall Lane (now Road), with the newly founded chapel of St. James at its centre.

By 1830, however, all these first-generation suburbs were either swamped or threatened by the spread of industry and less prestigious housing. The peace and tranquility of Bordesley, for instance, was disturbed not only by the cutting of the Warwick canal through its undulating pastures, but by the 'long streets of New Deritend' (Bradford Street, Cheapside and Moseley Street), which skewered it to the town. Even worse, in Drake's *Picture of Birmingham* (1831), we read that 'the ancient mansion' there, 'called the Ravenhurst, has been sacrificed to the Mammon of the day, and gives its name to "Ravenhurst-street", and space for brand new double lines of low-rented houses'.

Francis Dobbs, the early nineteenth-century comedian, summed up this inevitable – and oft-repeated – process with admirable clarity:

> I remember one John Growse,
>   A buckle maker in Brummagem:
> He built himself a country house,
>   To be out of the smoke of Brummagem:
> But though John's country house stands still,
>   The town itself has walked up the hill,
> Now he lives beside a smoky mill,
>   In the middle of the streets of Brummagem.

73

Only in one area would John Growse have been safe. This was at Edgbaston, where the Gough — Calthorpe family, who owned the estate, refused to allow the building of warehouses or factories. And indeed, a fair proportion of the pre-1830 development here — along the Bristol Road as far as Sir Harry's Road, and the Hagley Road as far as the Plough and Harrow — has retained its 'Roman cement' and superior status right down to the present day.

Government, Politics and Society

Apart from Sutton, which at Bishop Vesey's behest had received a charter of incorporation in 1528, local government throughout the Birmingham area remained in early Georgian times, as it had been for centuries, exclusively an affair of manor and parish. For a rural community of 500 to 1,000 souls this system still worked reasonably well. But for a busy industrial town, which by the 1760s had swollen to 30,000 inhabitants, it was totally inadequate. Nevertheless down to 1769 the structure of Birmingham's local government was no more than that of a market village.

In traditional rural communities the most important administrative function of the manor was the regulation of the agrarian economy. In Birmingham it had long been the control and supervision of retail trading, which was the responsibility of a Court Leet. This body elected annually a Low Bailiff, who nominated jurors, and therefore in effect controlled the composition of the court; and a High Bailiff, who presided at meetings, was chief market officer and inspected weights and measures. Among other leet appointments, the two Flesh Connors, or Low Tasters, kept watch over the sale of meat, while two Ale Connors, or High Tasters, had to see that the 'Publick Brewers and Ale Sellers . . . do brew good and wholesome drink', and that alehouse-keepers prevented 'tippling or gaming at their houses by apprentices or others'.

All these officers served on a part-time and unpaid basis; and so did those controlled by that other local government body, the parish vestry. The two constables and one headborough (elected by the leet, but financed by, and therefore answerable to the vestry) had the unenviable task of policing the town; the four surveyors of the highways of maintaining its roads in a state of good repair. However, expenditure under both these heads generally fell between £100 and £200 in the mid eighteenth century, and this gives some idea of the

limitations of the services provided. By far the most expensive branch of parochial government was the relief of the poor. This invariably cost in excess of £1,000 per annum from 1746 onwards, and by the early nineteenth century had risen to anything between 20 and 60 times that amount. As in neighbouring parishes, the tasks of collecting the poor rate and dispensing relief were in the hands of overseers of the poor. But in 1783 overall control of Birmingham's poor law administration was transferred from the parish vestry to a Board of Guardians; and from then onwards increasing use was made of salaried officers.

Thus reformed, and given the circumstances of the time, the administration of the poor law could not perhaps have been much improved; and market surveillance seems also to have been reasonably satisfactory. With the rapid growth of population and trade, however, market accommodation was urgently in need of extension. And, unlike the old market village, one of the country's most populous industrial towns could hardly manage for ever without adequate provision for such vital urban services as refuse removal, street drainage and street lighting. The intention of a committee of leading townsmen who in 1768 petitioned Parliament to authorize it to undertake such tasks was that Birmingham should no longer have to do so.

The resulting Improvement or 'Lamp' Act, as it was popularly called, nominated 50 Town Commissioners – later increased to 75, then 89 – with powers of levying a rate for the cleansing and lighting of streets, for the regulation of traffic, the removal of obstructive buildings from the centre of the town, and for transferring the cattle market from High Street to Dale End. Subsequent acts, passed between 1773 and 1828, authorized this body, among other things, to supplement the work of parish constables by employing a large body of night watchmen, to take over road maintenance from the surveyors of the highways, to initiate Birmingham's first smoke abatement scheme, as well as to provide the town with its Public Office, the Smithfield (cattle) Market, and ultimately the Market Hall and Town Hall.

The Street Commission was not a democratic body. Its original members were named in the 1769 Act, were not subject to removal, and themselves nominated persons to fill vacancies. As one critic wrote, they 'worked in the dark, unseen by the public eye and irresponsible to the public vote; they appointed their own officers, levied taxes at their pleasure and distributed them without check or control'. Nevertheless by 1830 this oligarchic body had enormously improved the cleanliness, security and appearance of the town; and thereby done much to bridge the gap between an outmoded semi-feudal system of local government and the rule of a modern-style municipal borough.

In the days of *laissez-faire*, it was no fault of the Street Commission that other public services — like the provision of hospitals and schools — which today fall within the purview of local government, then had to be left to the initiative and generosity of private individuals and voluntary bodies. The first medical provision in Birmingham, apart from the Workhouse infirmary, was the General Hospital 'For the Relief of Sick and Lame Poor'. This was inspired by the local physician, Dr. John Ash, built between 1766 and 1779, and financed by various fund raising enterprises which from 1768 included the Triennial Music Festivals. Medical services were further improved by the opening of a Dispensary in 1794 'for the purpose of medical relief to sick and midwifery patients of the poorer classes', if necessary, 'in their homes'. And before long the town also had an Institution for Bodily Deformity (1817), an Eye Infirmary (1824) and a Fever Hospital (1828), each of which was supported 'by the donations and annual subscriptions of its friends'.

Apart from the free grammar schools at King's Norton, Yardley, Sutton and Birmingham, the earliest educational institutions in the Greater Birmingham area were Charity Schools. These were generally founded under the auspices of the Society for Promoting Christian Knowledge 'to educate the children of the poor in reading, writing, moral discipline and the principles of the Church of England'. As it happens, one of the leaders of this movement, 'the indefatigable Dr. Thomas Bray', was rector of Sheldon from 1690 to 1730, and predictably the earliest local school was founded there in 1704. The Birmingham Blue Coat School was opened on the eastern side of St. Philip's churchyard in 1724, while other charity schools

Left:
The Bray Rectory, Sheldon.
Below:
The Royal School for Deaf Children, Church Road, Edgbaston. This was founded as the School for the Education of the Deaf and Dumb in 1812.

Holy Trinity Church of England Primary School, Bordesley. This was established in 1825 and the building erected in 1831. The legend above the window reads 'Sunday & Day Schools'.

were subsequently established at Northfield and Hall Green. Instruction in these schools appears to have been extremely limited, and probably few pupils did more than acquire some ability in reading. Certainly, half a century after the foundation of the Sheldon school, the majority of persons marrying in that parish were still unable to sign their name. During the period 1754-93 only 35 out of 104 did so. But there was improvement; between 1794 and 1812 of the 66 newly-weds 51 showed themselves capable of at least a signature.

A dissenting – as opposed to a Church of England – charity school was founded in Birmingham by the Unitarians of the Old and New Meeting houses in 1760. But after that – although the 25 private school teachers listed in a directory of 1770 must have catered for a considerable proportion of the town's middle class children – little seems to have been done to improve educational facilities among the poor until the early nineteenth century.

In 1809, however, a Lancastrian school was established in Severn Street for '400 boys of the labouring class'. Almost unbelievably, it had one master directing 'the whole school, through the medium of monitors selected from the boys'. 'This school', it was noted at the time, 'is supported mainly by Dissenters'; and the same commentator goes on to tell us that 'the National system was introduced to prevent the rapid progress the Dissenters were making'. The first three National schools, 'for the gratuitous education of the children of the poor according to the system introduced by Dr. Bell', were opened in Pinfold Street, Birmingham, Erdington and Handsworth, all in 1813. By 1830 there were similar institutions, among other places, at Ashsted, Bordesley and Yardley. Meanwhile the Birmingham Infant School Society had opened three schools in the town. These were to provide instruction 'to poor children of tender years . . . hundreds of which class are . . . neglected or left without proper protection while their parents are engaged in household duties, or in earning that income on which the subsistence of the family either wholly or partially depends'.

But the sum total of the above schools could have helped only a small minority of local children; and as late as 1840 it was stated – with or without an intended double meaning – that 'the Sunday schools of all denominations' were of greater importance as a 'means of acting beneficially upon the dense masses of the population'. The first Sunday School had been established in Birmingham in 1784, with the aim of removing 'labourers' children from noise and riot, and cursing and swearing' in the streets on Sundays. Similar institutions – often with their own buildings – were opened in considerable numbers during the early nineteenth century, the classes generally beginning at 8 a.m. and 2 p.m., with a programme that included reading, writing and arithmetic, as well as religious teaching. Some of these institutions eventually gave instruction to adults, while others developed into day schools of the National (Church of England) or British (nonconformist) variety.

This rivalry between Church and dissent, far from being confined to education, dominated every aspect of public life and local politics throughout the eighteenth and early nineteenth centuries. Well before the Civil War a strong Puritan tradition had been established in the town. Indeed, this was one of the reasons Birmingham – although not without its Royalist minority – gave such staunch support to Parliament against Charles I. Nevertheless, following the disappointments of the Interregnum, the Restoration brought a considerable revival of loyalist opinion among the local population: with the result that thereafter, for half a dozen generations, there existed a wide, perennial rift between, on the one hand, Church-Tory sympathizers, and on the other, those of dissenting and Whig persuasions.

Over long periods the merchants and manufacturers who controlled local affairs managed to hold this antipathy in check, their desire for compromise being epitomized by 'an unwritten but unbroken rule', which was probably established in the late seventeenth century, that the High Bailiff should be a churchman and the Low Bailiff a nonconformist. From time to time, however, feelings ran so high that this truce was temporarily violated. Thus, according to Hutton, a mob sacked the Digbeth Meeting House in 1709, and animosity against the dissenters again flared up in 1714 and 1715, at the time of the Jacobite rising. Sporadic riots against Wesleyans and Quakers in 1751 and 1759 kept alive the same vendetta, until it culminated in the infamous Priestley Riots of 1791. A dinner had been planned by a group of dissenting radicals to celebrate the second anniversary of the fall of the Bastille, and this sparked off several days of violence. Angry mobs, chanting such slogans as 'destruction to the Presbyterians', 'Church and King for ever' and 'no philosophers', destroyed or damaged one Baptist and three Unitarian meeting places, together with the houses of about a dozen prominent townsmen, including Joseph Priestley – who subsequently left for America – John Taylor II and William Hutton.

The fact that the Birmingham 'mob' seems invariably to have wielded its power against Radicalism and in favour of

Above:
The Destruction of Dr. Priestley House – from an engraving in Smiles Boulton and Watt.
Below:
In the year following the Priestley Riots a Barracks 'for 162 men and horse' was erected on the edge of the town at Ashsted. A road name still points to the site.

King and Church hardly suggests that there was a sharp sense of class consciousness among the inhabitants of eighteenth-century Birmingham; and neither does the comparative rarity of trade combination. Nailmakers were involved in a number of marches and protestations during the first half of the eighteenth century, while in the second half local filesmiths, buttonmakers, carpenters, bricklayers, tailors, brushmakers and shoemakers are known to have organized themselves, intermittently or on a more or less permanent basis, in the furtherance of trade disputes.

But a more characteristic type of 'working class' political action at this time was the food or bread riot, which generally involved small masters, as well as labourers and artisans – and indeed often enlisted the tacit sympathies of some of the big masters too. Such riots occurred, for instance, during the scarcity years 1756-7, 1762-3 and 1782; but they were at their most frequent and serious during the prolonged food shortage of the Napoleonic period.

A lack, or comparative lack of class consciousness is also suggested by the fact that when 'the rise of democratic feeling' did occur in the early nineteenth century – through the Hampden Club and the Political Union under Thomas Attwood – this took the form, not of a poor/rich rift within local society, but rather of 'a political alliance between working classes and middle classes'. Nor did this remarkable degree of social homogeneity go unnoticed by contemporary observers. 'The social and political state of that town', wrote Cobden in reference to Birmingham, 'is far more healthy than that of Manchester. There is a freer intercourse between all classes than in the Lancashire town, where a great and impassable gulf separates the workman from the employer'.

Cobden himself suggested one reason for this beneficent state of affairs: '. . . the industry of the hardware district', he says, 'is carried on by small manufacturers, employing a few men and boys each, sometimes only an apprentice or two; whilst the great capitalists in Manchester form an aristocracy'. What appears to have been another contributory factor was pointed out by W. Hawkes Smith in 1836:

> The operation of mechanism in this town, is to effect that alone, which requires *more force* than the *arm* and tools of the workman could yield, still leaving his skill and experience of hand, head and eye in full exercise; – so that Birmingham has suffered infinitely less from the introduction of machinery than those towns where it is, in a great degree, an actual *substitute* for human labour.

The skilled nature of the Birmingham labour force might have been expected to result in higher income levels than else-where; and indeed Thomas Attwood told a Parliamentary

Committee in 1812 that Birmingham workmen had been 'in the habit of earning more wages than fall to the lot of labouring men in general'. However, while Birmingham artisans earned, on average, about twice as much as local farm labourers, according to T. S. Ashton, the wages of men at Boulton's Soho Works were considerably less than those paid in Manchester mills. But more important than wage levels perhaps, or even than what we today would call job satisfaction, was the fact that the skilled Birmingham worker – by virtue of that skill and the comparatively small amount of capital required to start a business – could always nurse the hope of one day becoming a master himself. This social mobility, or as Asa Briggs has put it, this 'atmosphere which encouraged optimism about social mobility', was particularly stressed by Hutton. 'Many fine estates', he tells us, 'have been struck out of the anvil'; and to prove his point, he goes on to explain that out of 209 inhabitants who in his time 'possessed upwards of £5,000', no less than 103 'began the world with nothing but their own prudence'. By the same token – if only because of the violent trade fluctuations of the early industrial epoch – masters could fail in their enterprises. Hutton had seen 'Gunmakers roll in their carriages'. But he had also seen the 'chief magistrate . . . fall from his phaeton, and humbly ask bread at a parish vestry'.

Certainly, whatever the explanation, there seem no grounds for resisting the overall impression of another contemporary, that 'With the exception of the metropolis, there is perhaps no town in England where there are so many persons combining in themselves the characters of masters and workmen as in Birmingham, and none in which there is more desirable a chain of links connecting one with another'.

The Napoleonic Food Crisis

As a pre-industrial, and then only partially industrialized society, throughout the eighteenth and early nineteenth centuries, at least a third of all Englishmen – and perhaps nearer a half – lived permanently below, or close to, the 'primary poverty line' as defined by Rowntree. Nor can Birmingham itself, still less the surrounding rural parishes, be assumed to have provided exceptions to this sombre rule. However, the degree of destitution varied from time to time, the most crucial factors being the overall size of the country's population and the extent to which resources were available to support it. Down to 1750 it is unlikely that the economic wealth of England and Wales had ever been sufficient to sustain more

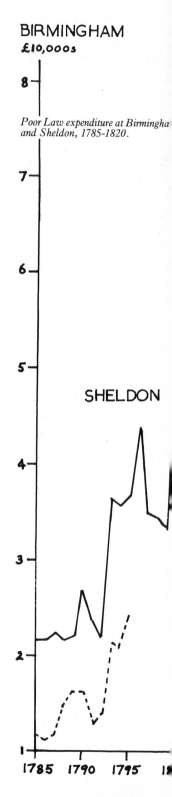

BIRMINGHAM
£10,000s

Poor Law expenditure at Birmingham and Sheldon, 1785-1820.

SHELDON

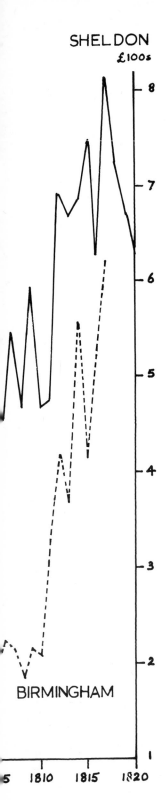

SHELDON
£100s

BIRMINGHAM

than about 6 million people. By 1801 the total population had risen to over 9 million. It was this almost too sharp demographic upsurge – plus the comparative difficulty of importing corn and exporting manufactured goods during the French Wars, and then the trade depression which followed – that created a twenty-five year long period of exceptional hardship and poverty for the working classes throughout England.

In the Birmingham area trouble began during the spring and summer of 1795. Due to drought, the 1794 harvest had been badly deficient. In fact, it was estimated that nationally the wheat yield averaged only 14 bushels per acre, as against 20 from the no more than satisfactory harvest of 1793. To add to the difficulties the subsequent winter of 1794-5 was exceptionally severe, and cool weather persisted through the spring and summer. On 29 June *Aris's Birmingham Gazette* reported: 'The great scarcity of grain which is experienced throughout Europe . . . has considerably advanced its price, and of course neither the same quantity of flour, nor the same weight of bread, can be afforded for the like money, as in more abundant times'. The same month brought scarcity riots in Birmingham. A mob, which included many women, forcibly entered a big steam-powered corn mill and bakehouse in Snow Hill; and contingents of Dragoons and yeomanry had to be called out to disperse the crowd, two persons being killed. As in earlier times of scarcity, steps were then taken to relieve the destitute, as well as to bring the unruly to justice. A soup kitchen was opened in Peck Lane, and a scheme launched to obtain emergency supplies of corn with the idea of making it available to the poor at subsidized prices. 'It is with pleasure', said *Aris's* on 13 July, 'we announce that a most liberal subscription is already begun in this town for the purpose of bringing to market a more ample supply of wheat and flour; and, we doubt not that every individual who has the means, will aid a subscription so benevolent and necessary'. Fourteen days later the same source reported that a Select Committee had 'applied to the Ports of Bristol, Liverpool, and Hull, for a supply of Corn' and had already 'actually purchased upwards of 3,000 Bushels of Indian Corn, part of which is arrived . . .'

Meanwhile, somewhat surprisingly in view of the cold summer, the 1795 harvest was expected to be good. And indeed, on 21 September we read: 'During the course of last week, the joyful sound of *Harvest Home* resounded at almost every farm in this and the neighbouring Counties; and we shall hope that all farmers will feel it their duty instantly to begin their threshing, and bring their wheat to the earliest markets, as a means of immediately putting an end to that great scarcity . . .'

81

However, in the event, the 1795 harvest proved to be little better than its predecessor; and wheat prices, far from falling, tended to move up still further. The national average price for 1794 had been 75s. (£3.75) per quarter; that for 1795 was 79s. (£3.95). Birmingham prices seem to have been well in advance of this. In July 1795, for instance, it was noted in the parish register of St John's Deritend that wheat sold for £1 a bushel. That was no less than £8 per quarter, or over twice the national average; and it would mean that the quartern white loaf (4¼ lbs), which had been 6d. (2½p.) in 1770, could not have cost less than 1s. 9d. (9p.).

After the 1795-6 peak, corn prices came down considerably in 1797, and remained at a relatively moderate level throughout 1798. But by the end of 1799 scarcity was again threatening. A riot against the price of potatoes is reported in February 1800, followed by bread riots in May and September. *Aris's Gazette* states that on 5 May 'a numerous body of rioters were gone to a respectable farmer's in the neighbourhood, threatening to burn his corn ricks'; but that 'troops were immediately despatched in pursuit of them, and came up just in time to prevent the execution of their purpose'. On the following Saturday 'everything was perfectly quiet', though 'the Yeomanry and Volunteers were all in readiness had it been necessary to call them out'. As before, in Langford's words, 'All that active charity could do to relieve the wants of the poor was done. Soup shops were opened; bread was sold to them below the market price; a collection was made in all the churches of the town in aid of the fund.'

Similar situations occurred in 1810, 1812, 1816, and worst of all in 1817 when the post-war depression was at its nadir. Despite the works of charity, it was the Board of Guardians who had to bear the main responsibility for relieving the destitute throughout this prolonged period of food scarcity; and in the poor law year 1817-18 their disbursement reached a peak of no less than £61,928. Moreover, according to Hutton's daughter, about 14,000 of Birmingham's 18,000 houses were at that time exempt from the levy. This must have meant that a mere 4,000 ratepayers had to produce the required total, at an average of about £15.50 each.

However, in absolute terms, the cost of poor law relief — and therefore, presumably, the degree of distress — was nothing like so great in Birmingham as in neighbouring rural parishes. On the basis of the 1821 census total of 85,416, the 1817-18 Birmingham disbursement represents an expenditure of £0.72½ per head of population. At Sheldon in the same year, with £813 being spent as against an 1821 census total of 423, the

The poor at the gates of the Birmingha(m) Workhouse. (from a print of c. 1830) The building was erected in 17.. and stood in Lichfield Street.

82

per capita cost works out at £1.92 — or 2.65 times higher than that for the industrial town. Put another way, this means that had Birmingham's poor law relief in 1817-18 been at the same *per capita* rate as Sheldon's it would have amounted, not to £61,928, but to £164,172. Again, in 1821-2, Birmingham had a *per capita* poor law expenditure of £0.52¼, Sheldon of £1,33½, which gives a virtually identical urban-rural differential of 2.56. During this same year, too, we know that 3,382 Birmingham inhabitants received relief, which was 3.95% of the total population. Sheldon's 87 recipients represented 20.6%. And when we bear in mind that a high proportion of paupers would have been receiving relief in respect, not of themselves merely, but of whole families, this must have meant that between a half and two-thirds of the Sheldon community needed some degree of parochial support.

In 1815 John Wedge, a Bickenhill man, wrote to the Board of Agriculture on the condition of the Warwickshire farm worker as follows:

> The weekly wages of an agricultural labourer are, at an average, not more than 12s. . . . The family of such labourer generally consists of himself, his wife, and from two to six children; when, out of this 12s. per week, he has provided fuel, clothing, and also shoes, candles, soap, salt, and beer (if any beer he can obtain), all of which are heavily taxed; and likewise set apart from 6d. to 1s. per week house rent, it will be perceived that, in very few instances, so much as 3d. a day for each one of his family can be spared for food, to support this indispensable class of society; but all deficiencies have been made up, either by the bounty of their employers . . . or by poor rates . . .

If local agricultural labourers were earning a mere 12s. (60p.) per week, it is not to be wondered at that they needed more from the parish rates than the Birmingham industrial worker. According to *Aris's Gazette*, 'one man haranguing the [Birmingham] mob' in May 1810 was heard shouting 'I can earn five and twenty shillings a week, and that is not sufficient to support me'.

Without question both the labouring and the artisan classes suffered almost unspeakably during this dreadful period. And we also have to bear in mind that countless people would have married, raised their families, and seen their children married in turn, without knowing any other conditions. Nevertheless, in the context of the times, this was a *nearly* tragic, rather than an absolutely tragic life-situation. For as we have seen (pages 43 and 67), in 1613-17 and 1727-9, when high corn prices threatened the poor with starvation, they had indeed starved. Or at least, they had died of malnutrition and its associated dysenteries and fevers. Those, surely, were the truly tragic times. By contrast, between 1795 and 1820 — essentially because of the fundamental economic strength and resiliance of a by now rapidly industrializing Birmingham and nation — we know that the poor, however much they may have suffered, did *not* die of starvation. For whereas at Yardley in 1727 and 1728 burials had multiplied three-fold, throughout the whole of the twenty-five year long Napoleonic crisis, mortality shows no upward tendency whatever — either at Yardley or in any other local parish. The overseers of the poor were busy, but not the sexton and clerk.

We know this. And perhaps the artisans of Birmingham who had actually to live through these desperate times — or at least some of them — knew it too. On 17 June 1812 'At a numerous and respectable Meeting of the Artizans of Birmingham . . . "to consider the best Means of expressing their Gratitude to those Gentlemen of Birmingham who have so laudably exerted themselves to restore the suspended Trade, and also to those who have so benevolently subscribed to the relief of the Poor of this Town"', one of the unanimous resolutions read as follows:

> That they who endeavour to promote the Commercial Prosperity of the Country, upon which its Welfare and Happiness so materially depend, deserve the lasting gratitude of the People.

The Town in the 1820s

The Birmingham of the 1820s, for all its rapid industrial growth and mushroom-like urban expansion, was still poised, as it were, between ancient and modern, between the Birmingham Leland visited and that of Joseph Chamberlain. Industrially the town was already staking out its claim as one of Britain's principal engineering centres — if only through Boulton and Watt's steam engines which were renowned throughout the kingdom. Yet with its countless small-scale and often ephemeral metal fabricating enterprises, in other ways it remained very much 'the hardware village'. So far as communications are concerned, canals encircled and criss-crossed the town, but railways had not arrived. The same betwixt and betweenness applied institutionally, socially and politically. Despite the fact that it was by now the third largest provincial town in England, Birmingham's local government — as we have seen — had progressed less than half way towards that of a modern industrial city. Poverty had only recently declined from pre-industrial levels. And although the town had since 1774 'justly assumed the liberty of nominating one of the representatives of the county' for Parliament, not till the 1832 Reform Bill would it be empowered to elect two M.Ps. in its own right. This transitional

Above:
The Bull Ring in 1829.
Left:
Swan Hotel (1829).
Below:
Theatre Royal (1829).

state — between old and new, 'pre-industrial' and 'industrial' — was clearly manifested in the physical appearance of the town.

A visitor in the 1820s would have looked in vain for the Old Market Cross or the Welsh Cross. Yet in place of these two early public buildings, the town now boasted about two dozen more recent and more imposing edifices, including the Public Office in Moor Street, hospitals, schools, libraries, a Gallery of Arts, even philosophical and literary institutions. And if a Town Hall and Market Hall were still lacking, by the end of the decade both of these would be in prospect.

The laying out of the open Smithfield Market on the levelled site of the de Birmingham moat by the Street Commissioners in 1816, as well as removing farm animals from the streets, had provided more space for retail trading. Nevertheless on Thursdays and Saturdays, we read in Drake's *Picture of Birmingham* (1831) 'the triangular area' of the Bull Ring was 'crowded nearly to the top'. Different parts were 'by common consent appropriated to the sale of different articles', and the scene was 'one of great throng and animation'. Even 'the causeways attached to the churchyard' were 'filled with small dealers . . . with exhibitions of books, stationery, white mice, and singing birds', together with 'large parterres of crockery ware'.

In the streets themselves, if cattle and sheep were now rarely seen, the same could not be said for horses. Apart from the endless procession of carts and waggons that graunched their way into and through the town, Drake speaks of 'the perpetual arrivals and departures of the numerous stage coaches, especially at about eight o'clock in the morning'. In fact, the 1820s brought 'the grand climateric of the coaching era'; and this meant that the old coaching inns were still extremely prominent. Among the best known of these busy and noisy establishments were the Hen and Chickens in New Street and the Saracen's Head in Bull Street. But the main concentration was along High Street. Here was the Swan, with its large open inn yard, the Nelson (which had just changed its name from the Dog, because of its position opposite the recently erected Nelson statue), the Albion, the St George's Tavern and the Castle. 'This is a locomotive community', exclaims Drake. 'Who that calls to mind the two or three night, or rather *night and day* coaches, which, in the first year of this century, travelled at a moderate pace, to and from London, would have conceived it possible that they should, in so short a time, have multiplied to at least *twenty*, running daily on the same route, with vastly increased speed?' Using the 'London Day Coaches', we are further told, the traveller 'may see the light of the same day in Birmingham and in London'.

The town's most fashionable thoroughfare was New Street.

Entering it from High Street, says Drake, 'the Hen and Chickens Hotel is the first striking object', with its 'projecting portico . . . *loaded* with balustrades and ornamental urns'. On the other side of the broad roadway was a line of shops and showrooms, including that 'of Mrs Bedford, for glass and china ware', which was 'adorned by a magnificent frontispiece of the Corinthian order'. A little beyond, and also decorated with a classical facade, was the Pantechnetheca. In effect this was Birmingham's first exhibition centre, where 'articles of Birmingham manufacture of ornamental construction' were permanently displayed, including 'jewellery, plate and plated goods, papier machée wares'. Further along New Street, too, 'the eye feintly catches a succession of good buildings and groups, among which are the Theatre, Post-office, and Society of Arts'.

Following its rebuilding in 1820, New Street's Theatre Royal could seat 2,500 people and was claimed to be 'one of the most superb Theatres out of the Metropolis'. However, we are also informed that its productions, which were often 'assisted . . . by Metropolitan performers', 'deserved better success than has generally rewarded them'. With its firmly established Triennial Music Festival and many music clubs, there appears no reason to doubt the contemporary statement that 'music was ardently and highly cultivated in Birmingham'. But drama does not seem to have fared so well. In fact until 1807 even the theatre in New Street was not legally licensed for theatrical perform- ances, and could offer only a summer season. The former circumstance was due to religious opposition, and to overcome it, the device had to be adopted of staging plays free during the interval between two parts of a truncated concert. Earlier theatrical ventures in Moor Street and King Street had long since lost their battles against dissenting opinion altogether. So much so, that both the theatre buildings concerned had been turned into nonconformist meeting houses. On the opening of the Moor Street theatre as a Methodist chapel in 1764 Wesley

Above left:
Old Meeting House, Cannon Street
Meeting House, Livery Street Meeting
House.
Above:
Christ Church, St. Thomas's Church.
Left:
Plaque in Ladywell Walk.
Below left:
The upper part of New Street in 1829.
Below:
A Georgian pub on the corner of Price
Street and Lower Loveday Street.
Below right:
Waterloo Street.
Far right:
Old Library, New Library, Birming-
ham News Room.

had declared, 'Happy would it be, if all playhouses in the kingdom were converted to so good an use'.

The most cursory inspection of the town would have confirmed the strength of dissent. In 1830, as against 12 churches, two Roman Catholic chapels and one synagogue, there were no less than 20 nonconformist chapels and meeting houses. However, if nonconformity had been able to check the development of the theatre, it seems to have made less headway against that 'besetting sin of the eighteenth century', drink. The 'genteeler sort of people' amused themselves at balls, assemblies and subscription concerts; or in summer visited Ladywell, 'the most complete baths in the whole island', or the fashionable Vauxhall Gardens at Ashsted, perhaps to see a spectacular display of fireworks. But Hutton — leaving aside cock-fighting, dog-fighting and other cruel sports — says that 'the relaxations of the humber sort, are fives, quoits, skittles, and ale'. There were well over four hundred pubs or taverns in the town by the 1820s, together with almost as many retailers of beer. And while many of the former served as headquarters for the socially useful working-class rent, clothes, sick, funeral and clock clubs, they also ensured that even at a place like Soho, 'some of the best workers were helplessly drunk for many days together'.

Returning to New Street, despite its growing importance for shopping and business purposes, much of its upper end was still lined with 'pleasant, almost rural residences, with trees and grass plots'. It was only recently, too, that gas lights had been introduced here, and the roadway properly paved. At the beginning of the century, the whole of the triangular space between New Street, Colmore Row and Temple Street had still been 'garden ground'. But by 1813 Christ Church stood at the

point of the triangle, where New Street met Colmore Row, and a few years later the remainder of this last substantial remnant of open land in the middle of the town was under development, with Bennett's Hill being laid across it in one direction and Waterloo Street in the other.

The town's main subscription library, the Old Library (founded 1779), with its 30,000 volumes and circular reading room, was in Union Street. But during the 1820s the New Library (founded 1796) erected 'a neat and commodious building' in Temple Row, while the Birmingham News Room opened a purpose-built premises in Bennett's Hill, in order to make available 'all the leading London, Provincial and Foreign newspapers, together with Shipping, Commercial and Law intelligence'. For the rest, this exclusively stone and stucco area — much of which remains intact today — was devoted mainly to shops, banks, and to the 'private establishments' of professional people.

Edgbaston Hall and Park in 1829

Beyond the densely populated chess-board estates that surrounded Birmingham's 'central business area', the town was now about eight miles in circumference. Yet by no means all its 3,000 manorial acres had disappeared under bricks and mortar by 1830. This was because, like the medieval town, its modern extensions had been confined to the eastern part of the ancient manor. That left the whole of the Rotton Park area still open country, while the 787 acres of Birmingham Heath — which had not been enclosed till 1802 — was only beginning to attract attention.

What mattered was not boundaries — whether of manor, parish or county — but proximity to the town. Hence the vulnerability of Edgbaston. 'This was till lately', we read in Drake, 'a rural village, and its ancient Church and simply-railed Church-yard, maintained the sequestered and tranquil character of rusticity'. But by 1830 'improvement' had 'discovered and disturbed this retreat'; 'gay villas and mercilessly straight streets stalk up to the very precincts of the sanctuary'. Similarly, though less tastefully — due to proximity — the original Deritend bridgehead into the parish of Aston had by 1830 ballooned out to include much of the ancient manors of Bordesley, Duddeston and Nechells.

Aston itself, on the other hand, was as yet more than a mile away from the straggling outskirts of the town, and therefore remained a relatively peaceful village. Its fine old park was still intact; as indeed was Edgbaston Park, which had been landscaped for Sir Henry Gough by Capability Brown in 1776, and Moseley Park, landscaped by Humphrey Repton. As for the remoter parishes of the Greater Birmingham area, the attack on their

'sequestered and tranquil character' lay far in the future.

The last remnants of medieval open fields had been enclosed at Handsworth in 1793, at Erdington in 1802 and Saltley in 1817. Meanwhile, between 1774 and 1824, over 7,000 acres of common waste was enclosed in the Greater Birmingham area. The main places affected were: extensive commons in King's Norton parish (1774), Handsworth Heath (1793), Witton Common (1802), Perry Common (1814), Washwood Heath (1817), and more than 3,500 acres of 'commons, wastes and open fields' in Sutton (1824).

In the parish of Yardley, however, 233 acres of common-field land and 661 acres of common pasture remained open right down to 1847. And anything up to a hundred corn harvests were still to be gathered from many of Greater Birmingham's fields.

The Philosophy of Birmingham

William Hutton's *History of Birmingham* was written exactly two hundreds years ago. 'The first nine months of this year', we read under 1780 in his *Autobiography*, 'were employed in writing the History of Birmingham'. Hutton adds, '*Rollason* the printer was pleased with it, and shewed it to Dr. Withering, who pronounced it the "best topographical history he had ever seen"'. Today the supreme value of this work lies not so much in the information it contains — though from Restoration times onwards that is useful enough — but in the fact that its author somehow managed to capture the *genius loci*, the spirit of the place. And the remarkable extent to which his characterization of Birmingham and its people still seems to ring true, tends to confirm both its reliability and its historical relevance.

William Hutton, who was born at Derby in 1723 and served a miserable seven-year apprenticeship there as a 'stockinger', first came to Birmingham in 1741. Derby he dismissed as a place 'for which I had a sovereign contempt'; and he did not think much better of Nottingham, where he worked for an uncle for thirteen years. Nearer at hand, eighteenth-century Coventry and 'Nun-Eaton', which Hutton subsequently visited in quest of employment, belonged in his view to 'the dominions of Sleep', lacking 'that active spirit which marks the commercial race'. His first impressions of Birmingham were completely different:

> Upon Handsworth heath, I had a view of Birmingham. St Philip's Church appeared first, uncrowded with houses, (for there were none to the North, New Hall excepted) untarnished with smoke, and illuminated

with a Western sun. It appeared in all the pride of modern architecture. I was charmed with its beauty, and thought it then, as I do now, the credit of the place.

The ourskirts of other towns Hutton had seen 'were composed of wretched dwellings, visibly stamped with dirt and poverty'. 'But the buildings in the exterior of Birmingham rose in a style of elegance. Thatch, so plentiful in other places, was not to be met with in this'. But if Hutton was agreeably surprised by the physical appearance of the town, its people pleased him still more:

> They possessed a vivacity I had never beheld. I had been among dreamers, but now I saw men awake. Their very step along the street shewed alacrity. Every man seemed to know what he was about. . . . The faces of other men seemed tinctured with idle gloom; but here, with a pleasing alertness.

At the time, unable to get a job with any of the town's three stocking-makers, Hutton saw no alternative but to move on. But nine years later he returned to set up shop as a book-seller and book-binder, first in Bull Street, and from 1751 at the lower end of High Street. Not himself devoid of 'that active spirit' he so much admired in others, before long Hutton had married — at St Philip's of course — and extended his trade by developing what was in effect Birmingham's first circulating library, and then its first stationery business or 'Paper Warehouse'. Following an unsuccessful attempt to go into paper manufacturing, however, he built a house for himself at Bennett's Hill, Washwood Heath, and thereafter devoted most of his surplus energy to public service — as a Street Commissioner and a Commissioner of the Court of Requests — and eventually to 'the book and the pen'. Unfortunately, being a prominent dissenter, Hutton's services to his contemporaries and to posterity counted for nothing 'in the dreadful tempest of ninety-one', when both the High Street shop and his Bennett's Hill house were destroyed. But, unlike Priestley, Hutton was too attached to Birmingham to be chased away. Instead he reconstructed his properties and continued living and working here until his death in 1813, at the age of 90. His daughter Catherine wrote:

William Hutton at the age of 80.

> My father had lived to see himself twice in fashion in Birmingham. Till the riots he was courted and respected. For some time after the riots he was insulted. He was now reverenced and admired. Two portrait-painters in Birmingham, requested him to sit to them, and one of them placed his picture in the public library of the town.

Hutton considered that 'the spirits which haunt Birmingham, are those of industry and luxury'. 'The town was large, and full of inhabitants', he says, 'and these inhabitants full of industry'. He would have agreed with de Tocqueville, who wrote:

> These folk never have a minute to themselves. They work as if they must get rich in the evening and die the next day. . . . One only sees busy

people and faces brown with smoke. One hears nothing but the sound of hammers and the whistle of steam escaping from boilers.

It was the atmosphere of the place itself, Hutton believed — or at least the attitude of mind prevailing among its inhabitants — that induced this appetite for work. 'It is easy to give instances of people whose distinguishing characteristic was idleness, but when they had breathed the air of Birmingham, diligence became the predominant feature'. But why were Birmingham people so work-crazy? According to Hutton, there was one reason, and one reason only — 'the view of profit'. 'The view of profit, like the view of corn to the hungry horse, excites to action'. Or again, 'Wherever the view of profit opens, the eyes of a Birmingham man are open to see it'. To illustrate this proposition Hutton offers a specific example:

> In 1772, a person was determined to try if a Hackney coach would take with the inhabitants. He had not mounted the box many times before he inadvertently dropped the expression, "Thirty shillings a day!" The word was attended with all the powers of magic; for instantaneously a second rolled into the circus. And these elevated sons of the lash are now augmented to fifteen. . .

Nor was the Birmingham man content to earn enough money merely to keep body and soul together. 'A small degree of industry supplies the wants of nature, a little more furnishes the comforts of life, and a further proportion affords the luxuries'. It was 'the luxuries' that Birmingham people were after. And indeed, it was this quest for luxuries that kept the whole manufacturing system in motion.

> A man, by labour first removes his own wants, and then, with the overplus of that labour, purchases the labour of another. Thus, by furnishing a hat for the barber, the hatter procures a wig for himself: the taylor, by making a coat for another is enabled to buy cloth for his own. It follows that the larger the number of people . . . the more they supply the calls of others, the more lucrative will be the returns to themselves.

A certain profligacy might seem almost a requirement of this 'work-and-spend' economy. In any case, Hutton noticed it in the local character. 'The people of Birmingham are more apt to get than to *keep*', he says. 'Though a man, by his labour, may treat himself with many things, yet he seldom grows rich'.

> I well knew a man who began business with £1500. Industry seemed the end for which he was made, and in which he wore himself out. While he laboured from four in the morning till eight at night, in the making of gimblets, his family consumed twice his produce. Had he spent less time at the anvil, and more in teaching frugality, he might have lived in credit. Thus the father was ruined by industry, and his children have, for many years, appeared on the parish books.

Hutton, with his nonconformist background and 'quaint prolixity', was by no means averse to wringing a moral from such tales. Yet he never for one moment questions the effectiveness or desirability of the new manufacturing system itself. Others did. Robert Southey, for instance, who visited Birmingham in 1807, while confirming the broad pattern of Hutton's analysis, had a more critical attitude to it:

> ... I am still giddy, dizzied with the hammering of presses, the clatter of engines, and the whirling of wheels; my head aches with the multiplicity of infernal noises, and my eyes with the light of infernal fires, – I may add, my heart also, at the sight of so many human beings employed in infernal occupations, and looking as if they were never destined for anything better. ...
>
> Not that the labourers repine at their lot; ... incredible as it may seem, a trifling addition to their weekly pay makes these short-sighted wretches contend for work, which they certainly know will in a very few years produce disease and death, or cripple them for the remainder of their existence.
>
> I cannot pretend to say, what is the consumption here of the two-legged beasts of labour; commerce sends in no returns of its killed and wounded. Neither can I say that the people look sickly, having seen no other complexion in the place than what is composed of oil and dust smoke-dried. ..
>
> Think not, however, that I am insensible to the wonders of the place:— in no other age or country was there ever so astonishing a display of human ingenuity: but watch chains, necklaces, and bracelets, buttons, buckles, and snuff-boxes, are dearly purchased at the expense of health and morality: and if it be considered how large a proportion of that ingenuity is employed in making what is hurtful as well as what is useless, it must be confessed that human reason has more cause at present for humiliation than for triumph at Birmingham.

Hutton was not oblivious to the darker side of the local scene. He tells of Birmingham workers whose 'time is divided between hard working and hard drinking'; and adds that 'it is no uncommon thing to see one of these, at forty, wear the aspect of sixty, and finish a life of violence at fifty ...' He was also aware of the exploitation of labour: though interestingly, the one clear example cited in the *History* refers, not to Birmingham artisans, but to Black Country nailmakers. 'While the master reaps the harvest of plenty', he comments, 'the workman submits to the scanty gleanings of penury, a thin habit, an early old age, and a figure bending towards the earth'.

But despite such excesses and injustices, Hutton plainly regarded industrialization as advantageous to all sections of society. The 'laborious part of mankind' were 'the prop of the remainder', while manufacturers and merchants 'supplied thousands of that class ... with the means of bread'. He was convinced too, that thanks to recent economic developments, 'the necessaries of life abound more in this reign [of George III], than in that of Henry the Third'. For 'our commercial concerns with the eastern and western worlds' had caused 'the kingdom to abound in bullion'. And this, together with the accompanying 'improvements in agriculture', had created an 'extraordinary stock' that provided 'a security against famine, which our forefathers severely felt'.

> . . . The poor inhabitants in that day found it difficult to procure bread; but in this, they sometimes add cream and butter.
>
> Thus it appears, that through the variation of things a balance is preserved; that provisions . . . are more plentiful, and that the lower class of men have found in trade that intricate, but beneficial clue, which guides them into the confines of luxury.

With such opinions, Hutton remained an unqualified 'yea-sayer', believing in the new system, and in its future:

> It is easy to see, without the spirit of prophecy, that Birmingham has not yet arrived at her zenith, neither is she likely to reach it for ages to come. Her increase will depend upon her manufactures. . . .

Strangers might question the merits of industrialization. The Birmingham man would have none of it. Long before it became the faith of the nation, Birmingham believed in Progress. And when the 'new Social Gospel' eventually arrived, it grew out of this belief, rather than developing extraneously, or in opposition to it.

Birmingham's bald, almost unprecedented single-word motto 'Forward' was not adopted until 1889, when the town was elevated to city status. Yet it would already have been appropriate a hundred years before. Indeed, Hutton himself might have coined it.

And perhaps the roots of Birmingham's forward-looking philosophy − if this is not a contradiction in terms − go back further than that. Even as far as the transformation of a sandy little Domesday hamlet into a flourishing medieval market borough. In any case − for good or ill − this philosophy is still with us today. In 1976 Alderman Griffin was speaking with a long tradition behind him, when, on being questioned about his reactions to the National Exhibition Centre, he replied, 'This is us, this is Birmingham, this is big. . .'

Forward!

Select Bibliography

Beilby, Knott and Beilby, *An Historical and Descriptive Sketch of Birmingham, with some account of its environs* (1830).

British Association for the Advancement of Science, *Birmingham and its Regional Setting* (1950).

Chapman, S. D. (ed.), *The History of Working Class Housing, A Symposium* (1971).

Court, W. H. B., *The Rise of Midland Industries, 1600-1838* (1938).

Dent, R. K., *Old and New Birmingham* (1880).

Dent, R. K., *The Making of Birmingham* (1894).

Drake, J., *The Picture of Birmingham*, Second Edition (1831).

Gill, C., *History of Birmingham, Volume I, Manor and Borough to 1865* (1952).

Gill, C., *Studies in Midland History* (1930).

Hutton, W., *The History of Birmingham* (1781).

Hutton, W., *The Life of William Hutton, F.A.S.S.* (1816).

Langford, J. A., *A Century of Birmingham Life: or a Chronicle of Local Events, from 1741 to 1841*, 2 volumes (1868).

Little, B., *Birmingham Buildings: the Architectural Story of a Midland City* (1971).

Pevsner, N. and Wedgwood, A., *The Buildings of England: Warwickshire* (1966).

Rowlands, M. B., *Masters and Men in the West Midland Metalware Trades before the Industrial Revolution* (1975).

Showell, W., *Dictionary of Birmingham* (1885).

Skipp, V. H. T., *Discovering Sheldon* (1960).

Skipp, V. H. T., *Medieval Yardley* (1970).

Skipp, V. H. T., *Crisis and Development, An Ecological Case Study of the Forest of Arden, 1570-1674* (1978).

Stephens, W. B. (ed.), *Victoria County History of Warwickshire, Volume VII, The City of Birmingham* (1964).

Index

References associated with illustrations are indicated by an asterisk.